INSTANT DECORATING

INSTANT DECORATING

Diane Henkler

Meredith® Press
New York, NY

To my mom and dad, Raymond and Genevieve McCoach,
who gave me the confidence to use my creativity
and nurtured it throughout my life.

———————————————————

Published by Meredith® Press
150 East 52nd Street
New York, NY   10022

Meredith® Press is an imprint of Meredith® Books:
President, Book Group: Joseph J. Ward
Vice President, Editorial Director: Elizabeth P. Rice

For Meredith® Press:

Executive Editor: Maryanne Bannon
Associate Editor: Carolyn Mitchell
Copy Editors: Patricia E. Pollock; Carol Anderson
Production Manager: Bill Rose
Art Director: Howard R. Roberts
Photographer: Julie Maris Semel

ISBN: 0-696-20330-8
Library of Congress Catalog Card Number: 92-077579

Printed in the United States of America
10 9 8 7 6 5 4 3 2 1

Acknowledgments

Without the help of many supportive people my dream of writing this book would never have become a reality. My sincere thanks to . . .

My husband, Ed, who deserves an award for his devotion and patience. He never complained about cooking dinner, doing the wash, or having to face the supermarket with two small children on Saturday afternoons.

Kelly and Amanda, my precious little girls, who had cereal for dinner every night, and their understanding that Mommy had work to do.

Carol and David Duell, Laura McCoach, Greg and Chris McCoach, and Jane Henkler for all their enthusiasm and encouragement.

George McCool for his legal assistance.

Maryanne Bannon, my editor—and after this past year, friend—who guided me through the facets of publishing a book and helped me get through my first experience of writing a book with ease. Her confidence in my work and her phone calls of encouragement were always a source of inspiration.

Julie Maris Semel for her beautiful photographs of the interiors and projects, and her assistant, Brian.

Howard Roberts for keeping us all smiling through a week-long photo shoot, and his patience in answering all of my questions regarding the design and for layout of the book.

Carolyn Mitchell for her help in getting the rooms set up for the photography.

Pam Tarpey for letting me decorate her beautiful home to use in this book and for helping me complete many of the projects.

Special thanks to Betty Lydon at York Wallcoverings and Kristin Kelley at Waverly, who generously provided me with the beautiful fabrics and wallcoverings that grace the projects in this book.

Pottery Barn, Fieldcrest Cannon, Domestications, and Sturbridge Yankee Workshop for letting me use their products.

Karen Rieg, Norah Stewart, Mary Lynn Federici, Jill Clement, Kim Barrett, and Carole Yeager for letting me use their decorative accessories at a moment's notice. My mom and dad, once again, and Jill Barcsz, Kathy Gluck, and Angie Rosen for keeping Kelly and Amanda safe and happy while I was busy during the photo shoot.

To the staff at Meredith Press, who made it all possible.

Dear Reader:

According to Diane Henkler, there is no one correct answer to the challenge of sprucing up a room or a piece of furniture; there are many answers. Better still, she'll convince you that limited time and money pose no problem, only possibility.

   Instant Decorating is brimming with attractive and original projects sure to lead you to immediate success. The collection draws on some wonderful, easily available resources to rejuvenate any home, at any time.

   The inspiring color photos and straightforward diagrams and instructions will prepare you for making that transformation, including dozens of ideas for every corner of the house. We hope you enjoy the many quick decorating tips, tricks, and shortcuts garnered just for this volume. Diane and all of us at Meredith® Press invite you to roll up your sleeves and...improvise!

Sincerely,

Maryanne Bannon
Executive Editor

Introduction

*I*f you are like me, you love to make your home look as if it came from the pages of your favorite decorating books and magazines. You long to duplicate the window treatments, pillows, table and bed linens, upholstery and innovative touches in home furnishings you see as you page through the beautifully decorated rooms. You may find the treatments or accessories too costly to purchase, however, and chances are you probably don't have the do-it-yourself skills necessary to make them . . . or do you? When I worked as a retail display designer I learned to meet decorating obstacles with a small budget, no sewing machine, and limited time by taking an unconventional approach to decorating.

Whereas conventional interior designers have the luxury to search for just the right chair and the perfect accessory, as well as hire a seamstress, display designers must learn to rely on their ingenuity. They are not afraid to experiment and often accomplish decorating miracles by using only the materials available in a prop room—usually a random selection of accessories, hardware, fabrics, paints, and supplies. Display designers use simple, unconventional methods to minimize time, expense, and effort while creating current decorator looks. They have no preconceived ideas and never overlook the importance of the smallest detail. If there are no curtain rods in the prop room and a window treatment must be completed within an hour, a wire coat hanger may be enlisted as a viable substitute. Instant Decorating will show you how to develop your creativity and decorating style as well as how to use the ideas, tricks, and shortcuts I learned as a display designer to make your decorating dreams come true. Many believe that decorating a home requires adherence to a rigid set of rules, an idea which may hamper creativity. But decorating is not like mathematics, where there is only one correct answer. In decorating there are an unlimited number of answers.

As an alternative to making expensive purchases or adding structural changes to your home, Instant Decorating will show you how to use simple, adaptable pieces and other items that you love, while relying on inexpensive cosmetic changes. Along the way you'll be helping the environment by reusing items in new and different ways instead of discarding them.

Instant Decorating was written to inspire and assist you in realizing your decorating dreams now. The homes we love are the ones that are decorated to reflect our personality, family history, and lifestyle, not Louis XVI's. Most of all, I hope Instant Decorating gives you the confidence to use your creativity and imagination while finding your own unique sense of style. Starting with materials you already own and adding your personality and such extras as fabric, paint, and odds and ends, you will soon be able to convert any house into the home of your dreams.

Diane Henkler

Contents

CHAPTER ONE

GETTING STARTED

TOOLS OF THE TRADE

Having the right tools and materials on hand goes a long way toward enhancing the pleasures of any decorating project. My most indispensable decorating tool is my idea book. Keep a scrapbook of ideas inspired by visits to model homes, decorator show houses, and furniture showrooms, along with clippings that appeal to you from your favorite decorating magazines. The photos in wallpaper books also provide inspiring decorating ideas. I find that a photo album with self-sticking acetate pages makes a perfect idea book. It allows you to see everything in a particular category at a glance and to weed through every once in a while without disturbing what you want to keep. You should add a few blank pages for notes, sketches, and written ideas. Divide your idea book into sections using notebook tabs and dividers. Initial sections might be Windows, Walls and Floors, Furniture, Decorative Accessories, Entire Rooms, and How-to Instructions. Clip everything that appeals to you: designs, colors, furniture placement, even the smallest details.

An idea book will help you to discover your preferences and experiment with visualizing. It will help you to identify your true decorating style while improving on your weaknesses. If you can't coordinate colors well, then you should have a section that concentrates on clippings of rooms with colors you like. Then study how the colors are mixed and coordinated. The best way to find out what really suits you is to identify consistent elements in your clippings; this will help you to avoid costly mistakes. If all of your room clippings have blue walls, you would probably feel very comfortable in a blue room. An idea book will give you ideas when you need them and help you make the right choices.

Although you do not need all of the tools listed below for every decorating project, it is a good idea to become familiar with them. Get to know the owner or knowledgeable employees at your local hardware and home-improvement stores, and ask a lot of questions. Once you start acquiring tools, try to keep them together so you'll know exactly where they are when you need them. There is nothing more frustrating than not being able to find the right tool when you are trying to complete a project. I have my own toolbox that is separate from my husband's. I also have a room in my basement for my supplies. If you do not have an extra room, try to set aside a closet in a bedroom or a cabinet in your laundry room for your supplies. If you need a larger work surface, place a folded pattern cutting board on your kitchen table or bed. A friend of mine uses the guest-room closet as her craft and decorating supply area. She installed shelves along the wall from top to bottom. Her tools are kept together out of the way but are easy to find.

Everything listed here is readily available at most crafts, fabric, or home-improvement stores.

Basic Tools

Acrylic paints—two-ounce bottles in a variety of colors.

Cardboard—save large appliance boxes.

Clear fishing line—use to hang or tie objects invisibly.

Cordless power screwdriver/drill—makes drilling a hole and driving or removing screws fast and easy.

Craft knife—for cutting paper, cardboard, or acetate. Have a supply of replacement blades.

Cup hooks

Decoupage medium

Fabric stiffener—mix three parts white glue with one part water to make your own.

Foam double-stick tabs/tape

Foam paintbrushes—leave no brush marks on painted projects and are easy to clean.

Hammer

Large-eye sewing needle/yarn darner.

Nails—all sizes.

Needle-nose pliers—use to hold and twist wire and coat hangers into shape.

Paper hole punch

Push/map pins—use to hold fabric in place temporarily when draping on a window.

Retractable metal tape measure

Rubber bands

Safety pins/straight pins

Scissors

Screwdrivers—both flat and Phillips head.

Screw eyes

Six-inch sewing gauge—use to accurately measure folds on unfinished edge of fabric to make a finished edge or hem.

Spray adhesive—aerosol glue that sprays out a thin coat of adhesive. Ideal for adhering fabric or paper to a large flat surface.

Spray paint—easiest way to instantly revitalize almost anything.

Trimmings—ribbons, cords, embroidery floss, and yarn.

T square or carpenter's square—a T-shaped rule that allows you to cut or draw a straight and square line.

Twisted paper cord—paper ribbon that is twisted like rope. Once untwisted, it is great for making bows and decorating accessories. Comes in solid colors, patterns, and lace.

Utility knife

Wire cutters

Wire—green florist's wire works best. Twist ties from bread wrappers can be used to attach details to fabric treatments.

Essential Tools

These tools will probably be the most costly of all the materials you'll need for your decorating projects, but they will be well worth the expense. In most situations a substitute can easily be found for any of the supplies you do not have, but there are no adequate substitutes for the following tools.

Hot-glue gun: This is probably the most important tool to have. There are many different types, ranging from cordless to dual-temperature. You can use a glue gun to hang objects on the wall, secure items to another surface, or hem fabric. Objects fastened or secured with hot glue can be easily removed, leaving little or no damage. I recommend a dual-temperature gun. This gives you very hot glue for some projects and the option to work with materials, such as plastic foam, that can melt if the glue is too hot. You should also keep a supply of glue sticks available.

Staple gun: This is a heavy-duty stapler that can attach materials to wood. It is used to cover furniture and walls with fabric, hang cardboard valances, pictures, and even make a temporary seam. Keep an extra supply of heavy-duty staples available.

Tracing paper: Transparent paper is used to copy designs from fabric, wallcovering, tiles—even your dishes—for transfer to other elements in coordinating a room's decor. You can use the paper to make a rubbing transfer onto furniture. Enlarge or reduce the design on a photocopy machine if necessary. To make a stencil, replace paper in a copy machine with acetate sheets and copy the design. Then cut the design out with a craft knife. You will become an instant artist.

TRICKS OF THE TRADE

Sewing Machine Alternatives

There are many new products available that allow you to make fabric treatments without a sewing machine. They require an iron and can safely be washed. Follow the manufacturer's directions.

Iron-on adhesive: Available by the yard or in precut rolls of various widths in fabric or crafts shops. You can make finished edges, hems, linings, and rod pockets on fabric projects.

Fabric glue: Use in place of iron-on adhesive. Squeeze from a bottle or a tube.

Fusing Techniques

To cut strips from a yard of iron-on adhesive: Fold adhesive in half, then fold in half two more times. Make vertical cuts 1 inch apart. Unroll each strip. (**Figure 1**)

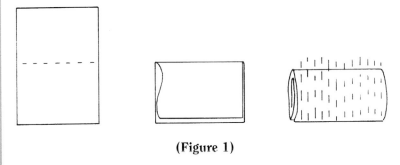

(**Figure 1**)

To make a finished edge or hem: Lay fabric right side down, fold raw edge of fabric over 1/4 inch and press. Fold again 1/4 to 1/2 inch and press to create a finished edge. Place a strip of iron-on adhesive or fabric glue along second folded edge and press to fuse. (**Figure 2**)

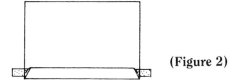

(**Figure 2**)

To line fabric: Lay fabric right side down. Fold all raw edges of fabric ½ inch and press to create crisp folds. Lay lining right side down. Fold and press only two sides (one length, one width ½ inch). (**Figure 1**) Lay fabric and lining with wrong sides together, so folded edges meet. Lay a strip of iron-on adhesive against edges or squeeze glue between folded edges and press. (**Figure 2**) Fold and press other two sides of lining over the fabric piece to match sides evenly. Tuck folds in between fabric and lining, place iron-on adhesive along edge, and press to fuse. (**Figure 3**)

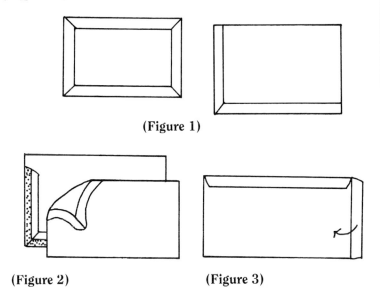

(**Figure 1**)

(**Figure 2**)   (**Figure 3**)

Seaming fabric: Lay fabric right side down. Fold sides of each piece of fabric to be seamed together ½ inch and press. Fuse together by placing a strip of iron-on adhesive between folds. Let cool and check bond. Press seam excess to one side. (**Figure 4**)

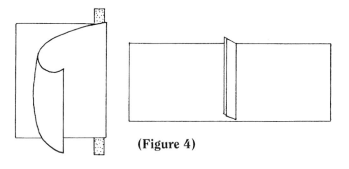

(**Figure 4**)

Fabric Tubes

Ruched cord cover: Cut cord to desired length. Cut a strip of fabric two times the length of cord by 4 inches wide. Lay fabric right side down. Fold one long edge of fabric over ¼ inch and press. Lay cord in center of fabric strip, bringing both edges over cord with raw edge of fabric underneath folded edge. Fuse with iron-on adhesive or fabric glue. Repeat until all fabric is on cord. Hold fabric on one end of cord with a pin. Push fabric cover back on cord to ruche. **(Figure 5)**

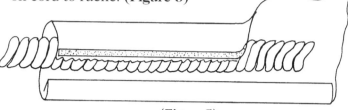

(Figure 5)

Tube of fabric for bows or rod cover: Cut fabric to desired length by two times the width. Lay fabric right side down. Fold over one long edge ¼ inch and press. Fold both long ends to center, overlapping slightly so raw edge is under folded edge. Fuse edges together. Tuck ends into tube of fabric ½ inch; fuse to make finished edges. **(Figure 6)**

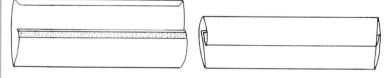

(Figure 6)

Gathering fabric: Sew a running stitch across the top finished edge of your fabric with embroidery floss or fishing line and a large-eyed needle. Push fabric back on floss to gather, tie fabric around project, and arrange gathers. **(Figure 7)**

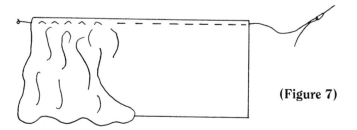

(Figure 7)

Other Nonsewing Options

Pins: Straight or safety pins can hold fabric on seat cushions and pillows in place. Also, use pins when a draped effect is desired on window treatments.

Bands: Use rubber bands to create poufs or rosettes in window treatments and table linens.

Staples: Make furniture slipcovers and chair-pad covers in a matter of minutes. Staples can even be used to hang window treatments.

Sticky back hook and loop fasteners: Can be hot-glued for extra hold to secure fabric instead of sewing.

Iron-on tapes: In window treatments use to make pleated and shirred headings.

Fabric Tips

- When choosing fabrics, buy the best you can afford. Get on your fabric store's mailing list so you'll know when decorator fabrics are on sale. Keep fabric width in mind. It is either approximately 44, 54, or 60 inches wide. It could make a difference in the amount of yardage you need. If you need two window treatments that require four yards of fabric for length but not for width, cut the four yards lengthwise to get two pieces. If you want lining, buy inexpensive cotton sheeting. Before cutting fabric, always ask yourself whether cutting the fabric in a different way would leave enough fabric for something else. Always save your scraps; they can be used to make decorative accents.
- Do not wash sheets or decorator fabrics. The stiffness creates a crisp look and holds poufs, rosettes, and folds in place. If fabrics do need to be washed, have them dry-cleaned instead or use starch to retain the body of the fabric.
- To cut a square or straight line in fabric, follow and cut along the repeat of the pattern or stripe. On solid-color fabric, use a yardstick and measure from selvage (manufacturer's finished edge) and mark your measurement; do this about every 12 inches for the entire length of the fabric. Draw a faint line connecting your marks and cut on line. On fabric with no

selvages or pattern, pull a thread from the fabric's length and width. Cut on pulled threads.
- To stop fabric from fraying, brush edge of fabric with a coat of fabric stiffener, let dry, then cut edge.

Painting Tips

- If it's clean, sanded, and primed any surface or object can be painted successfully—even Formica and ceramic tiles. There are many new products on the market. Ask at your paint store.
- Use a medium grade of sandpaper on a shiny surface to roughen it up so paint adheres better.
- Use a primer. If you are painting over a glossy or oil-base paint with latex products, use a "gripping primer" made especially for using latex paints over oil or alkyd types.
- If an object has a varnish or stain and you want to paint over it, sand it lightly and apply a "stain killer." If you don't follow this step, the stain or varnish will bleed through and discolor the paint. Ask for details at your paint store.

Professional Tips

- Hide staples by painting the top of a row of staples, using paint to match fabric. Let dry, load into staple gun.
- Cover staples already visible by hot-gluing a ribbon over them to create a nice border.

- Keep a cup of cold water handy when you are using a hot-glue gun to cool your fingers in case you accidentally burn yourself.
- Put a little hot glue into a hole that is too big for a screw so the screw will stay put.
- In the glove compartment of your car keep a plastic bag with window and room measurements, a tape measure, and fabric swatches from your upholstery and window treatments. This will allow you to determine exactly what you need to complement your décor while you are out shopping.

Points to Remember

When planning your decorating, always remember to:
- Forget all decorating preconceptions you may have.
- Realize that you do not have to take the conventional route. Improvise!
- Be observant of everything around you, even if it is not related to decorating, and see how you could adapt it for your home.
- Start an idea book.
- Break the rules and mix styles, periods, and patterns.
- Personalize your projects with details.
- Develop your own unique decorating style, trust your instincts, and become comfortable with your judgment.
- Experiment!
- Remember, there is always a way to get the job done successfully.

CHAPTER TWO

LIVING ROOMS

*T*he rooms we live in most should be a visual expression of our taste and lifestyle. If you conform to decorating trends and decorate a room as a "package deal," it will lack what is most important—your personality. You could be left with an outdated decor and no foundation for a new look when the trend fades. Trends in fashion and colors change frequently, with Southwest big one year and the rustic look the next. By understanding what true style is and being able to distinguish it from fashion trends, you can learn to vary your decor with current accessories rather than incurring the enormous expense of changing it completely. Geraldine Stutz once said, "The difference between fashion and style is that fashion says, 'me, too,' while style says, 'only me.'" Decorating with a personal touch that is unmistakably yours will outlast any trend. Designer sheets are fashion. It is how you use the sheets that gives your decorating true style. Keep abreast of what is new on the market, and scour flea markets, tag sales, and antique shops so you can find new ways to express your style. To begin, start off with a foundation of good-quality but basic pieces of furniture. Work slowly and build your room a piece at a time so you buy only things that you absolutely love. When you take the time to sit in the room that is undergoing a change, you can better visualize what it needs to make it a room that reflects your taste and personality. One of the living rooms photographed in this book has been interpreted four ways—with a different decorating style for each season. The classic sofa, wing chair, round table, lamp, bookshelf, and neutral background remain the same throughout each change. By changing slipcovers, decorative accessories, and shifting attention to details, I gave the room a dramatically new look while adapting to various decorating styles.

Spring—English Country

I chose an English Country look for spring because it reflects nature's renewal as well as our own. Flowers are blooming, birds are chirping, and color is sprouting up everywhere. We are bringing the outside in again, and our moods are bright and cheery after a dreary winter. A room that says English Country has plenty of color, flowers, and chintz. Florals, plaids, and striped fabrics are mixed in such a way that they blend harmoniously to create a formal coziness. Use tables and shelves to display your collections of pictures, books, and china. Warm up the spaciousness of the room with a needlepoint rug, and add a tray to the top of a small end table so that it resembles a butler's table. Use twice as many pillows on your sofa as you think you need, and sit back to enjoy afternoon tea.

Stapled Sofa Cover

When the upholstery on your sofa becomes faded, worn, soiled, or outdated, a new look can be achieved without expensive reupholstering or with the use of a casual throw. You can make an upholstered look by pin-fitting and sewing pieces of fabric together, then stapling the bottom edges taut to the underside of the sofa frame for a custom fit. Each cushion is wrapped separately like a package and secured on the underside with safety pins. Any type of fabric can be used. For a unique look, wrap each cushion in a coordinating fabric to add an appealing contrast. I found a very inexpensive denim that holds up to the wear and tear this sofa gets, while adding a splash of color against the white walls in the room.

Materials

Measuring tape	Safety pins
Fabric	Staple gun and staples
Straight pins	Clothesline for skirt
Iron-on adhesive	

1. To determine fabric yardage, first remove cushions. Measure the width of the sofa, starting at floor, up one side to top and down to seat, across full width of seat then up and down other side arm. To measure the depth of the sofa, start at floor, up front, across seat, up front of back, and down to floor. Add 2 inches to each measurement for stapling to underside of sofa. **(Figure 1)**

2. Measure each cushion separately to determine yardage. Measure width, length, and depth of cushion and double each measurement. Add 10 inches to each measurement. Measuring this way allows for extra fabric that will be needed to secure fabric to underside of cushion. **(Figure 2)**

3. You will be covering the sofa one piece at a time, pin-fitting each section together until the entire sofa is covered. Lay fabric right side down as you fit each piece. Start at the back and work out to the sides and front. If desired, when fitting arm section pin on matching or coordinating cord. **(Figure 3)**

4. Remove the entire cover and sew together. Trim excess at seams.

5. Turn to right side and place over sofa. Smooth fabric with hands.

6. Turn sofa upside down and staple fabric taut to underside of frame.

7. Cover each cushion by cutting out a square of fabric using measurements from Step 1. Fuse with iron-on adhesive to finish edges. Lay fabric right side down and wrap cushion as you would a package. Secure on underside with safety pins. **(Figure 4)**

8. For ruffled skirt, measure around the sofa and double the measurement. Measure from the floor to the part of the sofa where you want the ruffle to start, adding 2 inches for top fold and bottom hem. Fold top edge over 1 inch. Lay clothesline in and fold fabric over it. Sew clothesline in fold along entire length of fabric. Fold bottom edge over ¼ inch, then again ¾ inch and fuse. Gather fabric on clothesline and tie tightly onto sofa. Use hook and loop fastener to hold ruffle in place around corners.

Design Extra:
Lay a long lace table runner under cushions and let it hang over the front of the sofa as an accent.

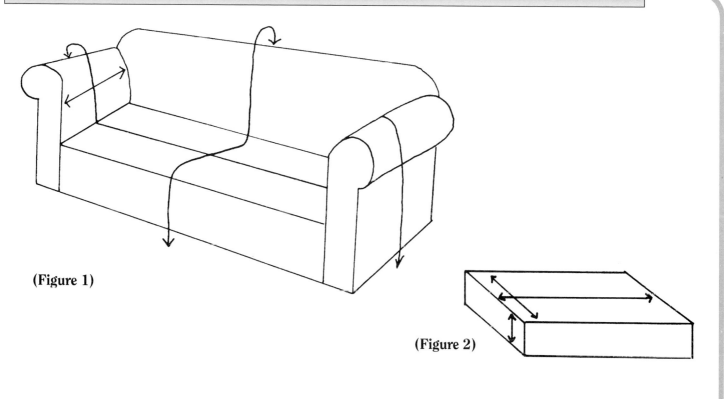

(Figure 1)

(Figure 2)

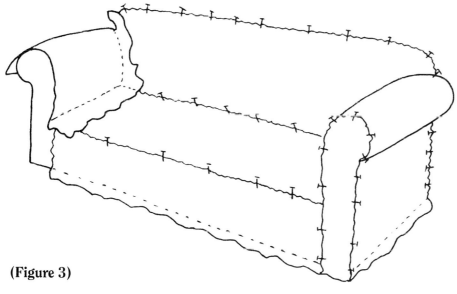

(Figure 3)

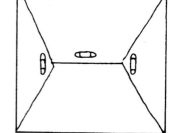

(Figure 4)

Tufted Ottoman

An ottoman is a versatile piece of furniture that can be used for more than resting your feet. It makes a colorful replacement for a coffee table, and can even be used as a seat for a cozy chat with a friend. An ottoman is mobile and will become a family favorite, especially if you attach casters to the bottom. Be prepared for squabbles about who'll get to use it. Have a clerk at the lumberyard cut your lumber to size and ask a friend to make an ottoman along with you. This way you will have an extra set of hands when needed to tuft the top. The floral and striped fabric and the ruffled skirt add to the English Country style of the room.

Materials

One 12-inch x 1-inch x 6-foot pine board	Eighteen ½-inch buttons
Eight 1-inch wood screws	Embroidery floss
Eight ½ to 1-inch wood screws	Large-eyed needle
Four 1-inch corner braces	Needle-nose pliers
One 28-inch decorator round tabletop	Staple gun and staples
5 yards fabric	3 yards stiff iron-on interfacing for skirt
One 26-inch square pillow	Iron-on adhesive or fabric glue
Straight pins	2 ½ yards of ½-inch cord
Pencil	Screwdriver
	Hot-glue gun and glue sticks

1. To make square base, have lumberyard cut pine board into two 16 ¾-inch pieces and two 14 ¾-inch pieces. Using 1-inch screws, attach boards as shown. Use two screws on each side. **(Figure 1)**

2. To brace square base, use ½-inch screws to attach braces to inside corners of base. **(Figure 2)**

3. Place table round on base and center. Using 1-inch screws, attach top to base. **(Figure 3)**

4. To determine button placement, center 1 ¼ yards of fabric on top of pillow. Temporarily pin corners to hold fabric in place. Measure 12 inches from each side to find middle. Mark with pencil. From center mark, make eight marks in eight different directions. **(Figure 4)**

5. To cover buttons, cut nine 1-inch-diameter circles out of fabric. Place button in center of wrong side of fabric. Thread needle with two 24-inch strands of embroidery floss and knot ends together. Sew a running stitch around fabric. Pull floss to gather fabric around button. Knot at button base, but do not cut floss from button or needle. **(Figure 5)**

6. To tuft pillow, place button on fabric-covered pillow. Push needle through fabric and pillow at center mark. The pillow is thicker than the height of the needle. This step is easier with four hands, so ask your friend to push the pillow down while you push the needle through the pillow. Use a pair of needle-nose pliers to pull the needle's tip through the pillow so you do not prick yourself. When the needle is out, thread it through the holes of an uncovered button. This will act as an anchor on the underside of the pillow. Have your friend press the pillow down while you pull floss taut. Sew on button and knot securely. Release the pillow. Repeat this procedure for all the other buttons.

7. Remove pins from fabric on pillow. Center tufted pillow on top of base and staple excess fabric to underside of round top. As you work your way around the top, make sure fabric is taut and pattern is straight.

8. The skirt is pieced together to save on fabric yardage. Cut four 13 x 54-inch strips from fabric and interfacing. Fold bottom edge of fabric pieces to make a ½-inch hem. Iron on interfacing to each piece. Fuse 13-inch sides of pieces together to create one long piece. Use floss to hand-sew a running stitch along the top to gather fabric. Tie around edge of round top. Arrange gathers evenly and staple to edge of round top. Trim excess. Cover staples with

2 ½ yards of ½-inch ruched cord. (To cover cord, cut three 3 x 36-inch pieces and follow the directions for making a ruched covered cord on page 14. Attach cord to ottoman with a hot-glue gun.)

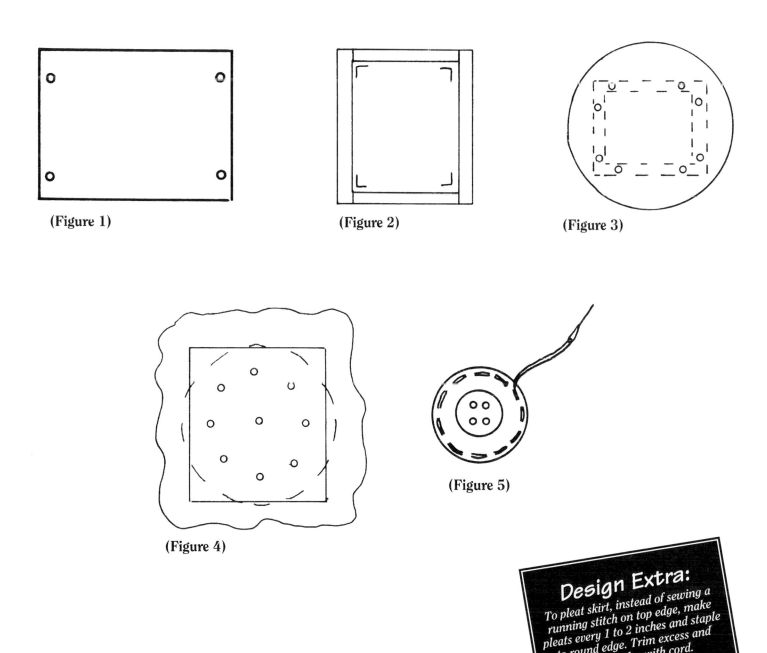

(Figure 1)

(Figure 2)

(Figure 3)

(Figure 4)

(Figure 5)

Design Extra:
To pleat skirt, instead of sewing a running stitch on top edge, make pleats every 1 to 2 inches and staple to round edge. Trim excess and cover staples with cord.

Ribbon-Woven Lampshade

As a display designer I was often called on to find merchandise that customers saw in a display but couldn't locate anywhere in the store. The customers frequently believed the item was sold out because the merchandise on display looked different—usually as a result of details I added to supplement the mood or theme of the display. When I pointed out the merchandise in the store's stock, customers couldn't believe that simply adding a decorative detail had changed the look so dramatically. Shifting attention to the details of a room not only enhances the overall appeal of the room but adds character, charm, and style as well. A plain lampshade becomes an eye-catcher when it is accented inexpensively with colorful ribbon. Choose a patterned ribbon or a solid color that coordinates with the window treatment or upholstery. Gaze around your room and try to visualize how your ordinary decorative accessories would look if you added a special finishing touch to them.

Materials

Lamp with shade
Pencil
Craft knife

Ribbon, double the bottom
and top circumferences of
the shade

1. Lay shade on its side. Starting from inside center front (opposite seam) and ¼ inch from the bottom, draw a vertical pencil line the width of the ribbon. Working toward the right, draw another line ¼ inch from the first line. Moving 2 inches to the right, mark a third vertical line. Then mark a vertical line ¼ inch from that line. Repeat, marking lines in this way until you reach the seam. Go back to center front and then mark shade to the left of center front. If there are any uneven spaces, they will be at the back. (**Figure 1**)
2. Cut lines with craft knife.
3. Weave ribbon through slits starting at seam, straightening ribbon out as you go. Knot excess on inside seam to hide and trim.

Design Extra:
Allow enough ribbon to tie a bow in front of shade. Start weaving from seam to each side to bring ribbon ends to center front; tie excess into a bow. Or weave entire shade, not just top and bottom edges.

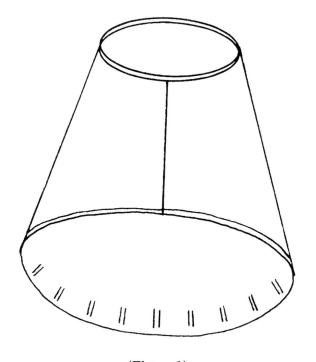

(Figure 1)

Fabric-Covered Lamp Base

Don't throw out a lamp because it no longer fits your decorating scheme or is chipped or just unattractive. Give it a new life by covering the base with fabric that coordinates with your new decor. If you need new lamps and are on a tight decorating budget, explore flea markets and yard sales to find unwanted lamps to cover. Find one in a size and shape you like and ignore its present exterior condition. Covering the lamp base is very easy and takes only about 10 minutes. During the holidays, use a festive sparkling or colorful fabric to cover your lamps and match the holiday theme.

Materials

Lamp	Ribbon or cord
Fabric	Hot-glue gun and glue
Craft knife	sticks

1. Center lamp base on a piece of fabric large enough to cover all sides of the base to just below the socket. Cut a small "x" with craft knife into fabric near base where cord is located. Thread cord through cut.

2. Gather fabric loosely around base. Arrange fabric so folds and gathers are evenly spaced around the lamp. Secure with ribbon at neck just below socket, or tie cord around neck and indents of lamp. Hot-glue cord ends in back.

Design Extra:

Measure fabric as directed then add a few inches more to the height. Line fabric with quilt batting. Wrap a rubber band around top of lamp base instead of using ribbon. Roll excess fabric down and tuck behind rubber band to form a ruched edge to the top of the covered base.

Poufy Tabletop

I love the versatility these inexpensive little tables offer when decorating a room. They are practical because they have hidden storage space underneath, are functional as tables, and offer a way to inject color and style into a room. When an attractive top is layered over the skirt, it adds depth and a pleasing contrast to the table. The poufs are quickly created by hand and evoke an English Country style that is reflected in the other elements of the room. To subdue the brightness of the yellow table skirt, lace curtain panels found in my attic were pinned under each pouf.

Materials

2 yards fabric
One 26-inch high decorator round table, 20 inches in diameter
Pencil
1 skein embroidery floss to match fabric
Large-eyed needle

1. Center fabric right side up on table over existing table-cloth. Make six small marks with pencil around top at even intervals. **(Figure 1)** Then make six corresponding marks on bottom aligned with top marks.
2. Thread about 20 inches of floss on needle and knot end. Starting from wrong side, sew a long running stitch from bottom mark on fabric to corresponding top mark. Bring needle to wrong side. Gather fabric on floss and tie end of floss to knotted floss on bottom. Trim excess floss. Repeat for each mark.
3. Tuck under excess fabric between each mark to make poufs. Arrange poufs so they drop to the same point.

(Figure 1)

Design Extra:
Hot-glue fabric bows around table to hide gathers.

No-Sew Round Pillow

Pillows are one of the most versatile decorating tools for shaping up a room and adding a quick splash of color. Whenever you buy fabric, be sure you buy enough to have remnants. I always make a point of buying more than I need just so I can add coordinating color accents to the smaller elements in the room. Covering a pillow with the same fabric used on the window treatments and placing it on the sofa balances out the cheery yellow used throughout the room. Round pillows stand out among mixed pillows of all shapes and sizes. Best of all, this unique cover requires no sewing or fusing and can be completed in a matter of minutes.

Materials

1 ¼ yards fabric
21-inch piece of string
Pencil
Scissors
16-inch round pillow or form
12 inches of ribbon
Fabric stiffener or white glue mixed with water

1. Fold fabric in half horizontally, then fold it in half vertically.
2. Tape end of string to pencil and hold string in top corner of folded fabric. Pull string taut and draw an arc on fabric. Cut through all four layers of fabric.
3. Lay fabric right side down. Center pillow and gather fabric around it. Tie with ribbon in front. Arrange gathers around pillow. Dab edges with fabric stiffener so edges won't fray.

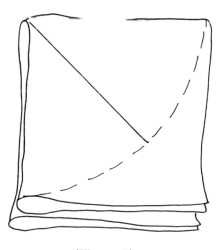

(Figure 1)

Plaid Pillow with Tassel

*I*f you can't redecorate but want to change the look of a room, try adding pillows of different shapes and styles on the sofa and chairs. By the time you finish, the room will have a new personality. The ruched edge already present on a solid-color ready-made pillow adds a decorator touch. Take it one step further by adding your own colorful fabric accented with shiny satin cord and tassel. There is no sewing involved, only iron-on adhesive or fabric glue. Pillows make thoughtful house-warming gifts because they add comfort and color to new and unfamiliar surroundings. The thought that you put into choosing a fabric to coordinate with someone's new home will make this a very special gift that looks as though you spent hours making it.

Materials

18-inch purchased pillow with ruched edges
½ yard fabric
½ yard iron-on adhesive

2 yards ½-inch multicolored cord
Tassel
Hot-glue gun and glue sticks

1. Measure center area of pillow, adding 1 inch to all sides. Cut fabric to size.
2. Lay fabric right side down. Fold over 1 inch on each side and press. Cut iron-on adhesive to same size as fabric. Iron onto wrong side of hemmed fabric. Remove paper backing. Center fabric right side up on pillow and press. Let cool.
3. Cut an 8 x 18-inch strip from fabric. Lay fabric right side down and fold long edges to meet in center, then fold strip in half lengthwise and press. Fold ends to back 1 ½ inches and press. Cut two small pieces of iron-on adhesive for each end of strip. Tie tassel onto center of strip. Press ends of strip to center area of pillow to fuse. **(Figure 1)**
4. Hot-glue cord onto pillow where ruched cord meets fabric. Trim excess cord. Hot-glue ends together.

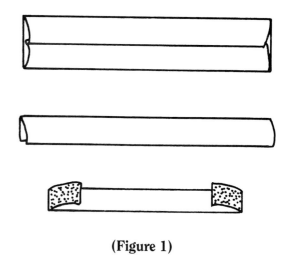

(Figure 1)

Tassels

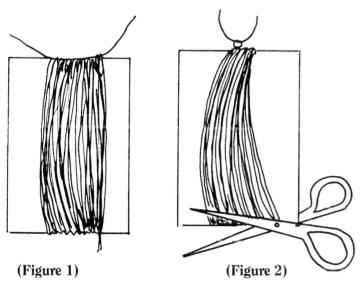

(Figure 1)   **(Figure 2)**

(Figure 3)

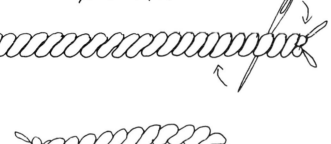

(Figure 4)

*T*assels are one of the easiest ways to add detail and color to any decor. Purchased silk tassels can be quite expensive and formal. By using different types of materials, however, such as embroidery floss, yarn, raffia, or even ribbon, tassels will look at home in a country setting. Add beads to the top or wrap a few identical tassels together for a unique larger tassel. I love to see tassels hanging from a book on a book shelf, furniture knobs, keys in keyholes, lamps, ceiling-fan pulls, and as drapery accents and tiebacks.

Materials

4–5 skeins embroidery floss, the more floss the fuller the tassel
Scissors
Cardboard, the length of tassel you desire
Needle

1. Wind floss over cardboard. **(Figure 1)**
2. With a 10-inch piece of floss, tie wrapped floss together at one end of cardboard. Cut other end with scissors. **(Figure 2)** Wrap an 18-inch piece of floss around tassel about ½ to 1 inch from top. Tuck ends under the wrapped floss with a needle or your finger. **(Figure 3)**
3. To make twisted cord for hanging tassels, unwind one skein of floss and cut into eight equal lengths. Knot together at one end and smooth strands of floss; knot other end.
4. Secure one end (I used a closed cabinet), pull taut, and twist opposite end with needle until floss begins to kink. Hold center of floss and remove end from cabinet, bringing the two ends together. Let go of the center and the floss will twist on its own. Knot ends together. Thread through top of tassel instead of using 10-inch piece of floss. **(Figure 4)**

Cardboard Shelf Backdrops

When I worked in display I think I covered more cardboard for backdrops than anything else. If your wall unit, hutch, or china cabinet lacks pizzazz, a backdrop can be wonderfully effective. Add color to it by covering cardboard from large appliance boxes with bright fabric. The backdrop will lighten up the shelf and highlight what it contains. A covered backdrop is a perfect way to make an unlit china cabinet look as if it is illuminated. Making backdrops for your furniture will help you repeat the color scheme while adding pattern to large areas where it may be needed for visual balance.

Materials

Fabric
Cardboard
Utility knife

Masking tape or heavy duty tape

1. To determine fabric yardage, measure height and width of each backdrop between shelves. Mark size on cardboard with yardstick. Cut cardboard with utility knife about ⅛ inch smaller on one side and top. The piece should fit snugly when covered with fabric.
2. Cut fabric 2 inches larger than cardboard on all sides. Lay fabric right side down. Center cardboard on fabric. If cardboard has any writing on it, place that side up. Tape edges of fabric to back of cardboard, making sure fabric is pulled taut. Fold corner fabric on the diagonal before taping.
3. Place in back of hutch. Repeat for all shelves.

Design Extra:
Cover books in a bookshelf with wallpaper from discontinued wallcovering books. Most stores will gladly give you the old books without cost.

Pattern Cutting-Board Fireplace Screen

1. Remove two panels from board with utility knife. This screen is only four panels wide.

2. Fold remaining board in half. Draw and mark pattern on two panels. Cut pattern out with utility knife. Fold the two cut panels onto uncut panels and trace outline; cut. **(Figure 1)**

3. Lay two rolls of gift wrap pattern side down on the floor. Use entire width from first roll of gift wrap for top portion of screen. You will only need a portion from the second roll of wrap to cover remaining bottom portion of board. If gift wrap has a pattern, make sure to match pattern at seam. Place cut board, plain side down on top of gift wrap and lightly trace outline of board with pencil. Draw second outline 5 inches outside first outline and cut the gift wrap on second line with scissors. **(Figure 2)**

(Figure 1)

(Figure 2)

F ew things provide a focal point for a room as effectively as a fireplace. If your home lacks one, consider faking it. This mantel is a family treasure that has been in my husband's family for many years and has graced many real fireplaces. I covered a plywood panel with fake bricks and placed it behind the mantel. It looks much like a real firebox. I wanted to purchase a very elegant screen, but it wasn't affordable. Instead I opted for "anything goes" and came up with a clever idea. I used a cardboard sewing board sold in fabric stores to make a decorative screen. The board is already folded and resembles a screen when placed on its side. Screens can be used to mask an empty fireplace in summer or a dirty one in winter. They can also be used to camouflage stereo equipment, unsightly walls, and radiators. Gift wrap comes in so many styles and colors there's sure to be one that complements your decor. And because the board and wrap are so inexpensive, the entire cost of the project is under $10.00.

Materials

Cardboard sewing board
Utility knife
Pencil

2 rolls of gift wrap
Spray adhesive

Design Extra:
Cover screen with wallpaper and border to coordinate with your walls or window treatments.

4. Turn cut board over and spray adhesive onto board and let dry until tacky. Carefully center top piece of gift wrap over board. Working from center out to all sides smooth out gift wrap to avoid creases and air bubbles. Repeat with second piece of gift wrap to cover remaining board.

5. Cut excess gift wrap as shown to wrap around ends. Spray adhesive on back. When adhesive is tacky, fold gift wrap over to adhere. Smooth with hands to flatten. **(Figure 3)**

(Figure 3)

Summer—Neoclassic

During the summer we relax, go on vacation and enjoy the freedom of the outdoors, but when the temperature soars, relief from the heat is also greatly desired. A neutral color palette can help make your decor visually cool on a hot summer day. Today's neoclassic style, which has its origins in ancient Greece, seems strikingly modern to our eyes and casts a fresh, clean, uncluttered look on your surroundings. Green topiaries and colorful flowers and fruits keep the neutral color palette from looking bland and boring by introducing accents of color to spark interest. The smooth texture of a glass-topped table, marble accessories, and urns overflowing with ivy feel cool to the touch. The sisal rug beneath unifies the room. Spray-paint your wrought-iron furniture and bring it inside. Use repetition as your decorating accent. Placing three of just about anything on a mantel, shelf, table, or wall creates eye-catching impact that looks elegant yet simple.

Sheet-Covered Sofa with Tassels

Our grandmothers used slipcovers to protect good furniture. Today we use slipcovers for more than protection. They give us the ability to dramatically transform a piece of furniture and change an entire room for the season or to unify mismatched flea-market finds and hand-me-downs. Sheets are an excellent choice for covering in the summer because the cool, crisp fabric feels better than wool or heavy upholstery. I chose a sheet with a neutral damask pattern to provide a touch of elegance to the neoclassic setting. To add distinctive style to a sheet-covered sofa, use decorative trimmings. Instead of using expensive cord, I opted for twisted paper cord to wrap around the sofa, then embellished it with a tasseled trim made from drapery tiebacks.

Materials

2 king-sized sheets to cover three-seat sofa	Waxed paper
⅜-inch-wide roll of iron-on adhesive	Wooden cutting board or flat work surface
Extra sheets to cover cushions separately	2 tasseled drapery tiebacks
Large safety pins	Fabric stiffener
Twisted paper cord, three times the circumference of the sofa	Straight pins
	Hot-glue gun and glue sticks

1. Remove cushions from sofa. With iron-on adhesive, fuse two kingsize sheets together at bottom hems with a ⅜-inch-wide strip of iron-on adhesive. Press seam to one side.

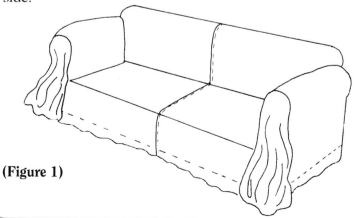

(Figure 1)

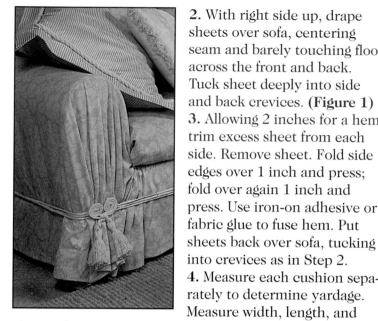

2. With right side up, drape sheets over sofa, centering seam and barely touching floor across the front and back. Tuck sheet deeply into side and back crevices. **(Figure 1)**

3. Allowing 2 inches for a hem, trim excess sheet from each side. Remove sheet. Fold side edges over 1 inch and press; fold over again 1 inch and press. Use iron-on adhesive or fabric glue to fuse hem. Put sheets back over sofa, tucking into crevices as in Step 2.

4. Measure each cushion separately to determine yardage. Measure width, length, and depth of cushion and double each measurement. Add 10 inches to each measurement. Cut yardage from extra sheet. (A king-size sheet will cover three cushions approximately 24" x 24" x 5".) Fuse to finish edges. Lay fabric right side down and wrap cushion as you would a package. Secure on underside with safety pins.

5. Place cushions back on sofa. Wrap cord around the sofa three times, below cushions. Use safety pin to attach cord ends under front arm on one side where tasseled trim will go.

6. To make coiled cord and tassels, lay waxed paper over wooden cutting board. Lay purchased tassel tieback down and flatten cord. Roll cord into circle. Generously brush on fabric stiffener. Push straight pins into coiled cord so it keeps its shape while drying. Repeat on other tieback. When dry, remove pins and waxed paper. Hot-glue onto each side of sofa. **(Figure 2)**

(Figure 2)

Sheet-Covered Wing Chair

A wing chair is a very traditional piece of furniture that might seem too formal for a neoclassic setting. But a knotted queen-size sheet placed over the chair transforms its fixed lines into a soft, more relaxed stance. The excess fabric is tucked into the chair's crevices. If you want the chair to appear more upholstered-looking, wrap the seat cushion separately and secure underneath with safety pins.

Materials

1 queen-size sheet
2 paper-towel tubes

1. Press sheet. Center over chair and tuck sheet in all crevices—back and sides of cushion. Put a paper-towel tube deep into seat crevices to hold sheet in place.

2. Knot excess sheet at corners. Arrange knots to hang gracefully, accenting the legs of the chair.

Design Extra:
Lay a long table runner horizontally or vertically over a plain chair to add contrast of color or to camouflage a soiled cushion.

Curtain Panels Plus

*T*oday's window treatments are often quite simple, allowing plenty of natural light to brighten our homes. Sheer white curtain panels are a timeless classic but may seem a little too plain on a rod by themselves. Change the way you style the curtain panels. Instead of tying back, pull them up and off to the sides of the window through spray-painted napkin rings to resemble a swag. The windows take on a subdued drama while admitting light and cool summer breezes.

Materials

Two 60 x 84-inch sheer curtain panels
Cafe-style rod
4 wooden napkin rings, spray-painted gold

1. For a single window, put curtains on rod and gather both panels to one end. Slide four napkin rings over opposite end of rod. Hang on window frame. Hold bottom of both curtains and gently pull curtains through napkin rings, letting ends fall to frame the side of the window. Spread curtain headings to hide rod. Pull curtain to desired swag drop and arrange fabric into graceful folds.

2. For a double window, use one long rod, four curtain panels and eight rings. Sweep two panels to the left and two panels to the right, as in the photograph.

Ruched-Cord Tabletop and Skirt

*F*or a neoclassic look a round table requires simple, clean lines. Ruched cord offers a decorative variation. The entire table cover is stapled onto a 20-inch round decorator table and requires no sewing. Cover extra-wide cord in a contrasting fabric to emphasize the decorative edge. The top is covered with glass to keep the fabric clean and add a cool surface. When it's time to change the skirt, the staples are easily removed with a pair of pliers.

Materials

3 yards decorator fabric
Staple gun and staples
⅜-inch-wide roll of iron-on
   adhesive or fabric glue
½ inch or wider cord, circumference of the table

Strip of coordinating fabric,
   4 inch by two times circumference of table
Hot-glue gun and glue sticks

1. To determine fabric yardage, multiply the circumference of the table by 2 ½ for the width and add 1 inch to table height for hem. For top, cut a square 2 inches wider than diameter of tabletop.
2. Lay square over tabletop. Staple taut to underside of table. Trim excess.
3. Lay skirt fabric right side down. Fold bottom edge and sides over ¼ inch and press. Fold over again ½ inch and press. With iron-on adhesive, fuse hem and sides.
4. Staple one top corner of fabric to table. Wrap fabric around table so fabric edges overlap slightly. Staple to edge of table. Fabric will drop to the floor from stapled ends. **(Figure 1)**
5. Pleat fabric at top; staple each pleat to edge of table. Work around table, making sure that pleats are even in size and spacing.
6. Cover and ruche cord. (See page 14.) Hot-glue cord around edge of table to hide staples with ends meeting in back. Tuck one end of fabric into the other and glue into place.

(Figure 1)

Wallpaper Pleated Shades

*P*leated shades offer an inexpensive and decorative option to plain miniblinds. They are also more economical to make than curtains, especially if you use leftover wallpaper. Pleated shades complement the clean lines of a modern room, yet their look can be softened by a fabric valance. To coordinate your room, try mixing solids, prints, and stripes using the companion wallpapers, borders, and fabrics from a wallpaper book. This project requires diligence and patience; give yourself about three hours to make your first shade; once you are familiar with the process, you will be able to complete consecutive shades in half that time. Work on a large clean surface, such as a kitchen table. The amount of materials needed depends on the size of your shade. To help visualize your shade, read all the instructions first, then draw a sketch of how your shade is to be constructed. This will give you a better idea of what your finished shade will look like and ensure professional results.

Materials

Wallpaper	³⁄₁₆ x 1 ¾-inch pine lattice
White glue	molding strip
Yardstick	½-inch screw eyes (very small)
Pencil	⅛-inch cord, approximately
Scissors or craft knife	10 yards for a 30-inch-
1-inch foam paintbrush	wide window
Paper clip	Cord cleat
⅛-inch paper hole punch	2–3 small angle irons or
(office-supply store)	wood screws to hang
Spray adhesive	shade to window

1. To determine amount of wallpaper needed, decide whether shade will be mounted inside or outside the window. Measure window width and length, adding 10 inches to the length.

2. If window-width measurement is wider than your wallpaper, you will have to seam pieces of wallpaper together with white glue. When seaming pieces of wallpaper together, the finished shade will look better if you center one full width of wallpaper and add a piece to each side. If your window is very wide, make two shades, placed side by side. Determine how many lengths of wallpaper you will need to cover the width of the window. **(Figure 1)**

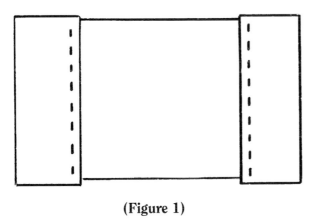

(Figure 1)

3. To cut side pieces straight, lay length of wallpaper pattern side up. From outer edge, measure half the amount needed to complete width of shade plus 1-inch for overlapping. Using a yardstick and pencil, mark that measurement randomly up the length of wallpaper. Connect all marks with yardstick to draw a straight line. Cut on line with scissors or craft knife. **(Figure 2)** On cut piece, make 1-inch marks randomly up inner edge on the length and connect with yardstick to draw a straight line. Do not cut. The pencil line will be your guide to evenly overlap wallpaper. Repeat for other side piece. **(Figure 3)**

4. To piece shade together, lay all pieces pattern side up. Spread a thin, even coat of white glue on the 1-inch overlap on each side piece with foam paintbrush. Place side pieces under center piece so edge of center piece just covers pencil line on side piece. Repeat on other side. Let dry.

5. To make pleats, lay shade pattern side down. Using a yardstick and pencil, mark length edges of shade in 1-inch intervals for pleat fold lines. **(Figure 4)**

6. Starting at bottom edge, connect first two marks horizontally across the shade with yardstick. Score by using the tip of an opened paper clip. Run the point gently against the yardstick. Match and score all marks. Scoring makes folding the pleats much easier. (Practice scoring on an extra piece of wallpaper; the amount of pressure needed varies with the thickness of wallpaper. You do not want to score through the wallpaper.) **(Figure 4)**

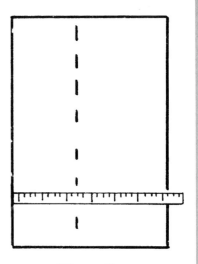

(Figure 2)

(Figure 3)

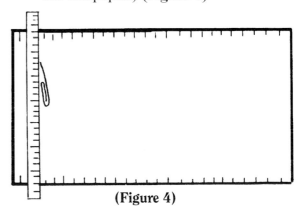

(Figure 4)

7. Accordion-fold the shade as you would a fan. After making each fold, run finger across fold, or lay fold over the edge of a table and press across fold to create crisp pleats.
8. To make hole punches, lay shade pattern side up. On bottom pleat, mark at even intervals across the width of shade where hole rows will be placed, no more than 25 inches apart. Pinch bottom pleat together on one side of shade. Punch a hole 1 inch from the edge. Continue working in this manner up one side of shade using previous hole punch as a guide. Two to four pleats can be pinched together to speed up the process. Repeat on other side and center of shade. Mark center row with a pencil first to make sure row is straight or follow pattern of wallpaper. **(Figure 5)**

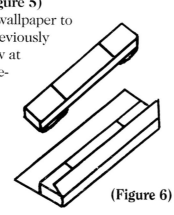

(Figure 5)

9. To mount boards, use extra wallpaper to cover two pine lattice strips, previously cut to the width of your window at the lumberyard. Use spray adhesive to adhere wallpaper to strips. Wrap strip ends first, then around entire strip with edges of wallpaper overlapping slightly. Let dry. **(Figure 6)**

(Figure 6)

10. Using spray adhesive, attach one covered mounting board to the top pleat and the other to the bottom pleat of the shade. Let dry. **(Figure 7)**
11. Lay shade pattern side down, align screw eyes on mounting boards to each row of holes, taking care not to screw through board. **(Figure 7)**
12. Each length of cord will be different. To attach cord, lay shade pattern side down. Start stringing cord from opposite side of where you want pull cord to hang. Knot cord on bottom screw eye and thread vertically through all holes, across the top through all screw eyes, and leave at least half the length of cord for the pull cord. Repeat for each row of holes. **(Figure 7)**
13. Attach cord cleat on the pull-cord side of the window.
14. To attach shade to window for outside mount, place shade on angle irons and screw in. For inside mount, screw mounting board to top inside molding of window from underside of shade.
15. Lower shade with cords and adjust cords to level shade. Knot cords together; trim excess. Wrap cord around cleat.

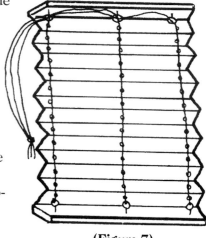

(Figure 7)

Design Extra:
Before folding shade for pleats, glue a coordinating wallpaper border to the bottom of shade. The full border will appear when the shade is closed, accenting the shade.

Shirred Lampshade

While transforming a room, don't neglect the smaller elements. Details are very important to the style and mood of a room. Make a simple yet stylish shirred lampshade to add a hint of color to a neutral palette. Shirred shades have clean lines to complement the simplicity of a neoclassic look. There is no extensive pleating or sewing involved; in fact, this shade was completed in less than 20 minutes. I made this one using fabric, gold cord, and hot glue. Choose a fabric and trim that repeats one or more elements in the room.

Materials

Lamp with shade	Clothespins
Fabric	⅛-inch cord by two times
Hot-glue gun and glue	the circumference of the
sticks	shade top

1. To determine fabric yardage, multiply the circumference of the shade bottom by 2 ½ for the width and add 1 inch to shade height.
2. Lay fabric right side down and fold all edges to wrong side, turning under ¼ inch. Make sure hemmed edges are straight. Press.
3. On front of shade opposite the back seam, place a short line of hot glue along top outside edge. Center fabric using this mark so the top edge of fabric aligns with the top edge of shade. Start pleating fabric around shade to right side, pressing pleats into hot glue to adhere. If necessary, clothespin pleats to hold until dry. Repeat from center to left side, overlapping in back where ends of fabric meet.
(Figure 1)
4. Pulling fabric taut, hot-glue bottom edge of fabric to inside of shade. Make sure fabric is evenly placed on inside of shade bottom as you work.
5. Wrap cord around the top of shade twice and hot-glue to adhere.

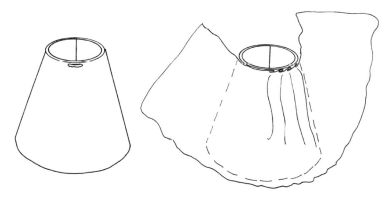

(Figure 1)

Gift Wrap-Covered Frame

I found a treasure one morning while I was taking my daughter to school. It was a large white picture frame with beveled edges, propped up against a garbage can. I saw beyond the chipped white finish. Hoping no one saw me, I picked up the discarded frame and drove off. I couldn't wait to get home and give it a new life with decorative gift wrap. I chose a gold damask-print gift wrap to resemble an ornate gilded frame I once saw. The gift wrap is cut to size and secured to the frame with glue. Accents in black, gold, or alabaster work beautifully in a neoclassic setting.

Materials

Picture frame	Paint, to coordinate with gift
Ruler	wrap for inner border of frame
Pencil	Roll of gift wrap
¼-inch-wide paintbrush	White glue

1. Remove any artwork and glass from frame. Using a ruler and pencil, mark a line ¼ inch from inside front edge of frame. Using pencil marks as guides, paint a ¼-inch gold border on the frame. If frame has beveled edges, follow beveled edge to paint an even border around inside of frame. Let dry. **(Figure 1)**

2. Measure and record each section of the frame: (A) length, (B) width, and (C) thickness—front inside edge around the outside edge to back inside edge. **(Figure 2)**

3. Using measurements, cut four strips of gift wrap to fit each side of the frame, adding 2 inches extra on all sides.

4. Fold 1/4 inch over on one long side of each strip, making a crisp crease.

5. Take one strip and center on one side of frame with folded edge just slightly overlapping where painted border ends. Cut the ends to follow the frame's diagonal and fit corners, leaving ½ inch extra to cover joints. **(Figure 3)**

6. When you are certain the piece fits, brush white glue on one side of the frame and place gift wrap on frame starting where painted border ends. Wrap the strip around the back and push any air bubbles out to the sides with hands. Cut away excess and fold edge to follow corner joint as if you were wrapping a package.

7. Repeat this process on opposite side of frame.

8. On adjacent sides of frame, repeat process, but fold ½ inch excess on diagonal cuts to create finished mitered corners in front and back of frame.

9. Return artwork and glass to frame and hang.

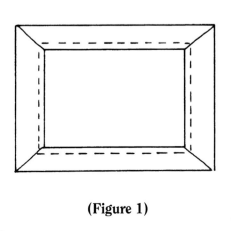

(Figure 1)

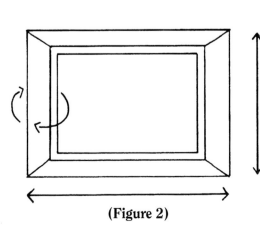

(Figure 2)

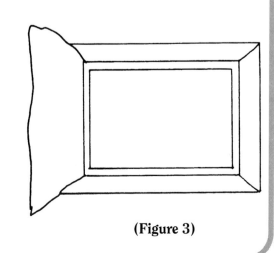

(Figure 3)

Flange-Edged Pillow

I never feel quite at home in a room without pillows. Besides adding comfort and color, pillows add visual contrast and depth to a large seating area. Choosing the right pillows is just as important as choosing the right lamp or chair. Although there are many styles of pillows to choose from, stick with simple shapes and trim in neutral colors for a neoclassical setting. Make a flange-edged cover with iron-on adhesive to give a small pillow a larger appearance. Accent the front by gluing on decorative trim.

Materials

Fabric	1 yard iron-on adhesive
Square pillow or form	½-inch cord, perimeter of pillow plus 1 inch

1. To determine fabric yardage, measure pillow and add 4 inches to each side. Cut two squares.

2. Lay one fabric square right side down and fold over all edges ½ inch; press. Repeat on other square.

3. Cut four strips of iron-on adhesive 4 inches wide and as long as one side of fabric.

4. Lay one piece of fabric right side down. Align the four strips of adhesive to outer edges of fabric square and press to adhere. **(Figure 1)** Remove paper backing on three sides. Lay second piece of fabric right side up on top of first piece, matching and aligning all corners. Press to adhere. Let cool.

5. Slide pillow in and fuse last side together.

6. Hot-glue cord around pillow form's perimeter to accent flanged edge.

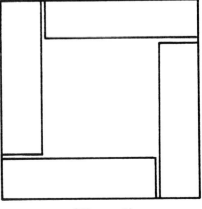

(Figure 1)

Autumn—Rustic

A mountain retreat or a love of nature makes one yearn for a rustic look. It's informal and a little rough around the edges, and it feels so comfortable. A rustic room doesn't have to be antlers mounted above the fireplace and fishing gear propped up in a corner. The rich, nubby textures from burlap, braided rugs, quilts, trading blankets, and crocheted accents soften the look that is dominated by elements from nature. An old chest without a lid is placed upside-down for a table in the center of the room. Baskets, dried flowers, rusted finishes, stoneware, and cast iron accessories finish the look.

Sheet-Covered Sofa with Bows

S lip on a new cover for autumn with sheets that reflect the vibrant yellow, orange, and rust colors the season brings. Decorative bows on gathered arms replace the formal tassels from summer to dramatically change the look of the sofa. The floral sheet sets the color scheme which is repeated throughout the room. Throw a soft afghan over one arm to snuggle under as the evenings become cooler.

Materials

2 king-size flat sheets
⅜-inch-wide roll of iron-on
    adhesive or fabric glue
Extra sheets to cover cush-
    ions separately (queen-
    size covers 2 cushions)

Large safety pins
12-inch sticky back hook
    and loop fastener

1. Follow Steps 1–4 on page 34.

2. From remaining fabric, cut eight strips of fabric 4 x 32 inches. Lay each strip right side down. Fold long edges on each strip to center, overlapping slightly. Fuse overlap with iron-on adhesive or fabric glue. Fold short edges over 1 inch and press to fuse with iron-on adhesive.

3. Gather fabric into even pleats on front of each arm and back corners. Temporarily pin in place. Cut hook and loop fastener into eight 1 1/2-inch pieces. Attach loop to one end of each strip on folded side. Attach hook to sofa cover, one in front midway between bottom of cushion and floor about 9 inches from sofa corner and one on the side about 4 inches from sofa corner. Repeat on other three corners of sofa. **(Figure 1)** Gather fabric into even pleats on front of each arm.

4. Attach strips to sofa and tie into a bow. Repeat on each corner.

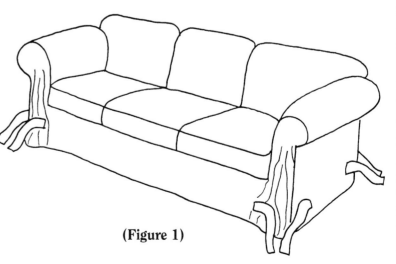

(Figure 1)

Design Extra:
Hot-glue sisal rope from a home-improvement store to the edges of pillows so they look at home in a rustic decor.

Burlap-Swaged Tree Branch

The fun of decorating in a rustic style is that the decorative accessories needed to adapt your interior are right outside your door. The best part is that they are free. Look through your backyard or nearby woods for tree branches the length of your windows. Modify by cutting off the smaller limbs, if necessary. You may even find branches in the shape of a Y. Cut these to about 6 inches high, screw or nail into the wall, and use as rod holders. I used large screws to hold the branch up. The silk foliage and birch branches add color and texture to the utilitarian burlap. This type of window treatment is perfect for a vacation home by a lake or in the mountains.

Materials

Burlap
2–3 large nails or screws, size 20d
Tree branch the length of your window plus 8 inches
Florist's wire
Raffia
Birch branches
Silk leaves in rust, yellow, red, and orange
Hot-glue gun and glue sticks

1. To determine the amount of burlap needed, measure length of window and double, plus 25 inches for each swag desired across top for width.
2. Hammer nails into wall or molding on each side of window. If you are working with a double window, place one nail in the center for extra support. Lay tree branch across. Tie branch on nails with wire.
3. Starting in center, tie burlap onto branch with strips of burlap or raffia. Let burlap dip across the window in poufs at even intervals. Let sides hang down freely to frame window, hiding nail and wire.
4. Arrange birch branches along top, tucked into tied strips of burlap. Hot-glue silk leaves on branch. Make sure you place leaves evenly across branch.

Design Extra:
Look for rolls of inexpensive burlap at garden-supply and home improvement stores.

Basket Lamp and Crocheted Shade Cover

A basket and a table runner are the easiest way to make a contemporary-styled lamp blend in perfectly with a rustic decor. Just place the lamp base in a large basket to camouflage the style and tie a cream-colored crocheted table runner over the shade. Try to find a basket that is as tall as the lamp base to hide it completely. Mixing the natural texture of the basket and the cotton fiber of the runner dramatically changes the lamp.

Materials

Large-eyed needle
Twine, raffia, or ribbon
Lamp
Basket

Crocheted table runner, two times the circumference of the shade bottom

1. Thread needle with twine, raffia, or ribbon and sew through pattern of runner along top edge. If runner is too long for the shade, fold the top edge over to shorten and leave as a flounce.
2. Tie crocheted table runner onto shade, tying twine into a bow or knotting and trimming excess. Arrange gathers evenly around shade.
3. Place lamp base inside basket.

Design Extra:
Cover a round table with burlap that puddles on the floor for a quick table cover. Finish top with a crocheted table round to accent.

Napkin Pillow

*P*illows provide an ideal spot to use a color or pattern that would be overpowering on a larger article. Colorful napkins are inexpensive and versatile pieces of fabric that make terrific pillow covers because of their finished edges. Best of all, when you get tired of the pillows you can use the napkins for dining again. You probably have cloth napkins hidden away in your drawers. You will need two napkins or scarves that are slightly larger than your pillow.

Materials

Pillow	Rubber bands
2 napkins	Raffia or ribbon

1. Center pillow between two napkins and tightly wrap each corner with a rubber band.
2. Cover rubber band with raffia.
3. Fold one edge of napkin under the other on all sides to partially close.

Design Extra:

For Turkish corner pillow, lay napkin right sides together and rubber-band each corner. Turn out. Fold pillow and squeeze through one side opening. Fold side edges one over the other to partially close.

Burlap and Raffia Pillow

A chair is just a chair until a decorative pillow is added for extra comfort and character. Burlap and raffia are two rugged textures. Together, they can make a plush pillow feel at home in rustic surroundings. You'll find both come in a wide variety of colors, so don't feel limited by the brown color. Use raffia or twine when decorating a rustic room where you would normally use ribbon to accent furnishings.

Materials

Burlap   Large-eyed needle
Pillow   Raffia
Twine

1. Cut burlap 1 inch wider than pillow on all sides. Using twine and needle, hand-stitch three edges together, leaving about ⅝ inch for seam. Turn right side out. Place pillow inside. Turn edges under about ⅝ inch and stitch closed.
2. Make four tassels from raffia. (See page 29.) Thread top two strands of tassel through burlap at each corner and tie on.

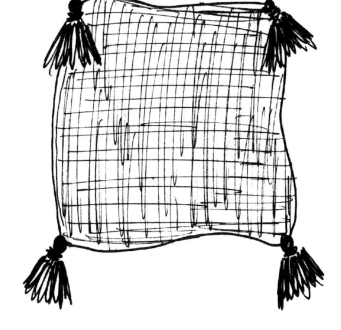

Design Extra:
The wing chair is covered with a strip quilt made using fabric scraps from the room's projects. Thrown over the chair, the quilt adds a rich medley of pattern.

Stitched Throw Rugs

*I*n addition to covering a floor, area rugs add color, texture, and warmth to a room. They can define space for smaller groupings of furniture in a large room and create balance throughout. Rag rugs are very inexpensive but are usually too small to cover a large area. By sewing two or more together, you get the feel of a larger area rug without the cost. The rug pictured in this Autumn living room is actually two long throw rugs sewn side by side. In the Winter living room (see page 52), there are three smaller rugs sewn side by side.

Materials

2 or more cotton throw rugs
Large-eyed needle
Embroidery floss to match
   rug or clear fishing line

1. Thread needle with floss or fishing line. Sew together rugs using a long overhand stitch. **(Figure 1)**
2. If the rugs have fringe along borders that will be sewn to another, turn fringe under before sewing.

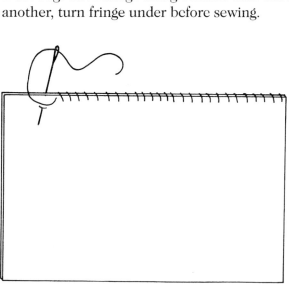

(Figure 1)

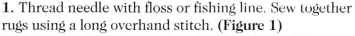

Design Extra:
Mix-and-match rugs of different colors and patterns to create a truly unique floor covering.

Winter—Traditional

*T*he time-honored pleasures of a traditional interior will never be out of style. The gleam of brass highlights the rich, dark hues of the tailored slipcovers and window treatments. Tartan plaids are an excellent fabric choice, and they mix well with linen slipcovers and fringed candlewick pillows. Black accents anchor the room and are carefully balanced throughout. Antiques, family heirlooms, a grandfather clock, and cherry wood make you feel welcome. When the winter chill arrives a warm and snug interior makes us feel securely sheltered from the frigid elements outside. Just imagine sipping hot chocolate by the fire, curled up on the sofa with a good book while the snow falls beyond the window.

Fabric-Covered Sofa with Pleated Skirt

Do you have your heart set on a certain fabric to change the look of your sofa but find reupholstering is too expensive? And using sheets as covers won't do? Worse yet, you have no sewing skills. Worry not—a cover can still be made with fabric, iron-on adhesive, and a little ingenuity. The fabric is pieced and seams are fused together then tucked into crevices and between cushions. The pleated skirt is an optional piece that requires sewing. If you want the cover to be permanent, use a staple gun or hook and loop fastener to attach fabric to the sofa's underside for a taut, upholstered look. The type of sofa you have will determine how easy it will be—a sofa that has no wings or curves will be very easy to work with.

Materials

Fabric
⅝-inch-wide roll of iron-on
    adhesive
1 yard sticky-back hook and
    loop fastener
Straight pins

Safety pins
Coordinating fabric
½-inch cord, circumference of
    sofa plus 4 inches
Hot-glue gun and glue sticks

1. Remove cushions. Measure sofa depth and length (see page 20). You will need approximately 16 yards of 58-inch-wide fabric for a three-cushion sofa.
2. From fabric cut two long pieces the length of sofa. Drape one piece starting at floor, over seat, and up back. Drape second piece from front over to the back to touch the floor. The seam will be running horizontally along the seat back. Fuse two lengths together with iron-on adhesive. Press seam to one side.
3. Cut two more pieces of fabric to cover arms, making sure each piece covers the arm and extends past arm the height of the sofa. **(Figure 1)**
4. Smooth fabric across sofa and tuck excess deep into crevices. Trim excess from all sides. Attach 1-inch sections of hook and loop fastener about every 12 inches to underside of frame and on wrong side of bottom edges of

fabric. Pull fabric taut and adhere to frame. Smooth fabric on back of sofa and wrap like a package at each corner, then attach to underside of frame. Arrange fabric into folds on the front of each arm. Place a pin on each side temporarily to hold folds in place.
5. Measure each cushion separately to determine yardage. Measure width, length, and depth of cushion and double each measurement. Add 10 inches to each measurement. Cut fabric, then fuse to finish edges. Lay fabric right side down and wrap cushion as you would a package. Secure on underside with safety pins.
6. For pleated skirt, measure the circumference of the sofa and multiply by 2 for the length. For width, measure from floor to bottom of seat cushion and add 1 ½ inches for top and bottom hems. Cut fabric. Fold top edge of long side ½ inch and press. Fold bottom edge of long side ½ inch and press. Fold bottom edge over again another ½ inch, fuse with iron-on adhesive, and press. Let cool. For cord cover fabric, the length is the sofa's circumference

measurement plus 4 inches; the width is 4 inches. Cut coordinating fabric to these dimensions. Cover cord by placing coordinating fabric strip around it. Glue fabric together or fuse under cord using iron-on adhesive.

7. Box-pleat skirt about every 2 inches and hold each pleat in place with straight pins. Sew across top and remove pins. **(Figure 2)**

8. Attach covered cord to top of wrong side of skirt. Sew onto skirt. **(Figure 3)**

9. Mark where skirt will be attached on sofa. Center pleated skirt on front of sofa. Starting from the center front, work to the left by placing a line of hot glue along sofa where marked a small area at a time and press top of cord over glue. Hold in place for a few seconds, then continue working in this manner around the sofa until you reach the back. Then go to the front and work to the right side until edges meet at the back of the sofa. Match edges and glue so edges butt against each other. Trim excess if necessary.

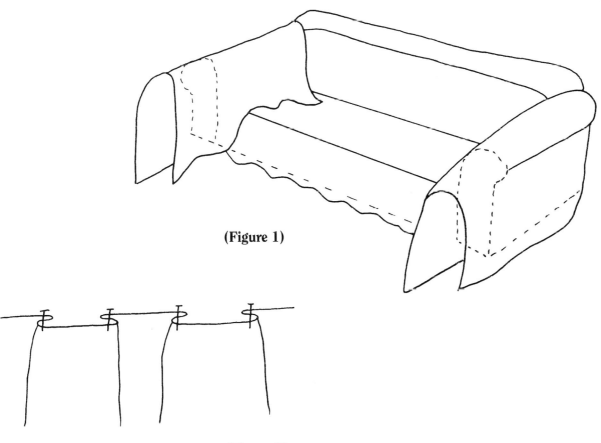

(Figure 1)

(Figure 2)

(Figure 3)

Fabric-Covered Wing Chair

Sheets are a great way to cover furniture, but they may not be available in the patterns you want. Fabric comes in a wider selection of colors and patterns, and fabric covers are just as easy to make when you call on the magic of iron-on adhesive. When choosing fabric for a winter room, the texture of the fabric is very important. Use linen or woolen blends to make the room feel warm, toasty, and tailored. The wing chair is right at home here and is covered now to disguise its color. This cover is no more than a throw that's wrapped with a belt to create a tailored look.

Materials

Fabric
3/8-inch-wide roll of iron-on
   adhesive
Straight pins

Sticky-back hook and loop
   fastener
3 paper towel tubes

1. To determine fabric yardage, you will need three pieces of fabric cut to the same length (depth measurement of chair). Measure full depth of chair beginning at floor, continuing up front, over seat, up chair back and down back to floor. To measure width of side pieces, measure from inside crevice of chair over arm and down to the floor. (The two side pieces will be the same width.) For center piece, measure across chair cushion at its widest part and add 10 inches. Cut each piece of fabric to above measurements. **(Figure 1)**

2. Lay center piece of fabric right side down and place a side piece right side down on either side. Using iron-on adhesive, fuse side pieces to center piece. Press each seam to one side. Fold bottom edge of fabric over ½ inch and press. Fold over again 1 inch and use iron-on adhesive to create a finished edge. **(Figure 2)**

Design Extra:
Make the wrap extra long and tie ends into a big decorative bow to accent one corner of the chair.

3. Center fabric over chair and bring finished edge to front of chair right above the legs, making sure to cover upholstery, smoothing fabric into seat back and side crevices to hide the seams in crevices. Smooth fabric around arms and let excess fall to sides. Mark the front with a pin for later re-positioning.

4. To make wrap belt, measure circumference of chair where cover will be tied, adding 4 inches. Using this measurement, cut fabric into a 5-inch-wide strip. Lay strip right side down and fold long edges into center, overlapping slightly. Fuse overlap with iron-on adhesive. Tuck short edges in about 1 inch. Fuse and press. Attach 2-inch hook of hook and loop fastener to right side of one end, then loop to the opposite end on wrong side. Wrap around chair, hooking in back.

5. Arrange fabric into gathers around corners and sides of chair. Make sure everything is smooth and pattern is straight.

6. Cut fabric on sides and back of chair 4 inches below chair upholstery. Remove cover. Lay cover right side down and fold three unfinished edges of fabric over ½ inch and press. Fold over again 1 inch and fuse with iron-on adhesive to create finished edges.

7. Using your pin as a guide, place cover back over chair and tuck excess into crevices. Smooth fabric over chair, making sure all upholstery is covered and cover lays evenly around chair. Attach wrap belt to hold cover in place. To keep fabric from slipping, place a paper towel tube deep into each crevice.

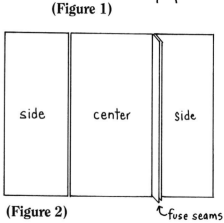

(Figure 1)

depth

side width

center width

(Figure 2)

| side | center | side |

fuse seams

Shirred Curtain Rod with Tennis-Ball Finials

When I decorated the windows for this Winter living room I had only one wooden rod from a yard sale. On the small window I used a cardboard tube that the fabric had been rolled on; luckily the tube happened to be the same diameter as the rod. I'm telling you this only to emphasize that any item can be used for decorating. Don't overlook anything, even if it seems far-fetched. Improvise! Anything that isn't visible can often be faked. Finials add dramatic accents to a window treatment and come in many different styles. Instead of purchasing them, save money by using tennis balls. The rod cover centered between the panels not only hides the fact that there is a cardboard tube in place of a rod but is an excellent way to add eye-catching detail with coordinating fabric.

rod cover over rod. Arrange gathers evenly on center of rod. See opposite page for curtains. Add one curtain to each end of rod; mount on brackets nailed to walls. Place covered tennis balls on end.

Materials

Fabric
Wooden pole rod, PVC pipe, or cardboard tube
Coordinating fabric
2 tennis balls

Utility knife
⅜-inch-wide roll of iron-on adhesive
Wooden pole brackets or 2–3 20d nails to hold up rod

1. To determine fabric yardage for rod cover, measure rod for length; width is circumference of rod plus 3 inches. Cut two 10-inch squares from coordinating fabric for finials.
2. Trace end of rod onto each tennis ball. Cut a hole in each tennis ball with utility knife using circle as a guide. Center a tennis ball on wrong side of one fabric square, wrap fabric around ball, then push excess into hole. Push curtain rod into covered tennis ball. Repeat with other tennis ball. If you want a larger finial, line fabric with quilt batting before wrapping around the ball.
3. To make rod cover, lay fabric right side down. Fold one long edge over ¼ inch and press. Fold both long sides to center, overlapping slightly so raw edge is under folded edge. Fuse with iron-on adhesive and press. Let cool. Slide

Design Extra:

Spray-paint large pinecones gold or white to resemble purchased plaster finials found in home-furnishing catalogs. Use hot glue or wire to attach the bottom of the pinecone to the end of the rod.

Flounced-Heading Curtains

I f you like the look of traditional curtain panels but want yours to look unique, add a flounced heading. It will add an unexpected frill to a room with traditional accents. I used linen fabric with a mixed paisley pattern and iron-on adhesive to make the entire curtain; no sewing was involved. The ribbon fused to the curtain's edge emphasizes the flounce and draws the eye while modifying the shape of an ordinary window. Letting curtain panels fall to the floor makes the window appear larger than it really is.

Materials

Fabric
⅜-inch-wide roll of iron-on
    adhesive

Pencil
4 yards ½-inch-wide ribbon

1. To determine fabric yardage, use the total width of fabric for each panel. For length, measure from floor to top of mounted rod, adding 10 inches for rod pocket, 8 inches for flounce, and 1 inch for hem.
2. Take advantage of fabric manufacturer's finished selvages by folding over and fusing with iron-on adhesive.
3. Lay panel right side down, fold top edge over ½ inch, and, press. Fold over top again 7 inches plus rod width; press. With a pencil, mark where top folded edge meets bottom fabric.
4. From mark, measure width of rod plus 1 ½ inches. Mark. Place ⅜-inch-wide strip of iron-on adhesive right above each mark. Press and then remove paper backing. Fold fabric over again, matching corners, and press. Let cool. **(Figure 1)**
5. To make flounced heading, fold fabric in half lengthwise. Draw a line from center out to side. Cut on line

through both thicknesses. **(Figure 2)**
6. Fold over each raw edge 1 inch and press. Put a ⅜-inch strip of iron-on adhesive between the folded top edges and fuse. Fuse ribbon with iron-on adhesive onto top edge of flounce, about ½ inch below top edge. Wrap ends of ribbon to back and fuse. Let cool. **(Figure 3)**
7. Hem bottom with iron-on adhesive. Push rod cover to center of rod and slide a curtain panel onto each side of rod. Place a covered tennis-ball finial at each end as directed on page 57.

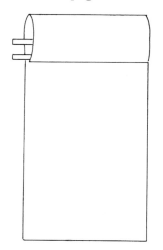

(Figure 1)

(Figure 2)

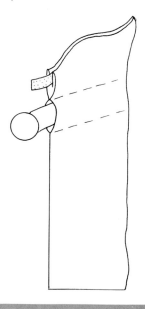

(Figure 3)

Doorknob Holdbacks

Using glass, ceramic, or porcelain doorknobs found in old homes, at flea markets, or garage sales is an excellent way to accent window treatments. They introduce a shiny texture that contributes to the window treatment's overall appeal. Holdbacks appear more formal than their tieback counterparts. What is especially nice about them is that they function with such ease, allowing you to just reach behind the curtain to release and close it and to simply place the curtain behind it to open. A tieback, by contrast, must be untied or unhooked every time.

Materials

2 doorknobs
Two 20d nails
Paint

Hammer
Hot-glue gun and glue sticks

1. Remove screw, shaft, and back plate from doorknobs if necessary.
2. A size 20d nail is needed for its length and support. If the nail head will not fit into the back of the doorknob, decrease size of nail head by hammering the head until it fits. Paint nail to coordinate with curtains and let dry. **(Figure 1)**
3. Hammer nail into wall where you want curtains to be held back, leaving about 2 to 3 inches of the nail exposed.
4. Use hot glue to secure doorknob over nail head.
5. Drape curtain over nail section, leaving doorknob exposed in front.

Design Extra: Make a ruched sleeve of coordinating fabric to cover nail instead of painting.

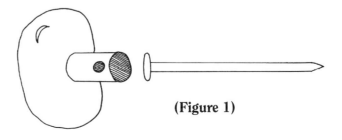

(Figure 1)

Pleated Lampshade Cover

Something as simple as a new shade cover and a brass pot can change a lamp's styling and adapt it to a traditional decorating scheme. Here, the new black shade is coupled with a tall brass pot covering the base, producing a warm glow. The black pleated shade is a cover for an existing shade and is tied on with satin cord. There is no special fitting or tying to a frame, which makes the cover a very easy way to illuminate a lamp with color. I used cotton chintz that is fused to interfacing then pleated. Shiny black cord is strung through small slits to tie the cover onto the shade. For added color you might want to try a bright ribbon.

1. To determine fabric and interfacing yardage, measure lampshade, add 2 ½ inches to height, and double circumference at widest part of shade for length.
2. Cut fusible interfacing to this size and press onto wrong side of uncut fabric. Cut fabric to same size as interfacing.
3. Lay fabric right side down. Fold all edges to wrong side 1 inch and press. Fuse with iron-on adhesive.
4. On wrong side use ruler and pen to mark every ½ inch for pleats along both long edges.
5. Connect marks with yardstick and accordion-fold as you would a fan. After making each fold, run fingers across fold or lay fold against the edge of a yardstick or table edge and press across to create crisp pleats. **(Figure 1)**
6. Cut a slit in the center of each pleat about ½ inch from top using craft knife. Thread satin cord through needle, then thread cord through each hole. Tie pleated cover onto lampshade so ends meet in back. Thread needle with black thread and run thread through all pleats about ½ inch from bottom. Place shade cover on lampshade and arrange pleats evenly around shade. Tie cord and thread into knot on inside of cover; trim excess.

Materials

Fabric	Yardstick
Lampshade	Craft knife
Heavyweight fusible inter-	⅛-inch black satin cord, cir-
facing	cumference of widest part
⅝-inch-wide roll of iron-on	of shade
adhesive	Sewing needle
Ruler	Black thread
Marking pen	

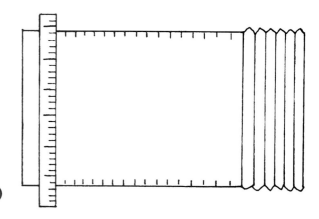

(Figure 1)

Stained-Glass Window Sash

An old window sash that I found in my neighbor's trash was the inspiration for this portable stained-glass window. Window sashes hung on a wall will resemble the real thing if you lack windows in your home. Place a mirror behind a sash and hang it across from a window. The light from the window will be reflected by the mirror, giving you the feeling of much more light. When you are scouting for sashes, look for those with unique shapes and a lot of detail. The stained glass on the window sash is not real stained glass but a product called Gallery Glass Window Color™ sold in crafts stores. The lead strips are made with liquid leading that you squeeze from a bottle and allow to cure before applying. The color is applied right from the bottle and smoothed out in various ways to achieve different effects.

Materials

Liquid leading	Tape
Window sash	Craft knife
Paint	Gallery Glass
Design, size of windowpane	Window Color™

1. Follow manufacturer's directions for making and curing liquid leading strips.

2. Paint window sash and let dry.

3. Draw or trace a design and tape it to back of one pane on window. Place liquid leading on front of glass following design; use a craft knife to cut leading to meet at corners. Repeat for each pane on window.

4. Apply window color according to manufacturer's directions. Let dry.

Design Extra:

Put magazine covers, calendar pictures, or your child's artwork behind each pane on the sash and hang like art on the wall. Each pane will act as a frame.

Window-Sash Table

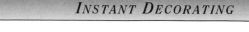

The idea of using a window sash and making a functional and decorative piece of furniture from it is recycling at its best. The idea is to use leftover lumber from a previous project. I used extra lumber from a new deck. Some knowledge of woodworking is helpful in completing this project (my dad helped me design and make this one). Look in your garage or buy an old sash at a salvage yard. I found mine in curbside trash. Look for interesting sashes to make your table truly unique. Glass kitchen cabinet doors from older homes are also terrific. If your sash is painted and you want to strip and stain it, experiment on the underside of the sash and wood first. Each section of wood might respond to the stain differently. The measurements for lumber are determined by the size of your sash. Note: The numbers in the illustration correspond to items in the Materials list.

Materials

❶ One window sash
❷ Four 1 ⅜-inch square
   balusters for legs (leg
   length plus thickness of
   sash should be approximately 18 inches high for
   coffee table or 21 inches
   high for end table)
❸ Two 1 ⅜-inch square balusters for cross braces
❹ One 1 ⅜-inch turned
   baluster for center brace
❺ 1 x 3-inch pine board for
   table rails, cut into 2 sections for short sides, 2
   sections for long sides
Drill
Clamp

Wood plane
Wood glue
Wood screws, #6 or #8 deck
   screws 2 ½ inches long
⅜-inch-diameter tapered
   hardwood plugs
Primer
Sandpaper, #80 grit
Foam paintbrush
Black semigloss enamel
Clear file folder or acetate
   to make stencil
Pencil
Gold stencil paint
Stencil brush
Masking tape
Fine-tipped black marker

1. Prepare surface of sash by removing hardware and planing millwork if necessary. Sand surface until smooth.
2. The length of all lumber for legs and cross braces is determined by the width of the sash and whether you are making a coffee table or end table. The length of the center brace will be determined by the length of sash. Cut all lumber to size. **(Figure 1)**

3. Assemble end frame first, making sure frame is square by laying legs and cross braces on a flat work surface. Use a spacer to support the upper rail during assembly. Clamp the frame into position, checking for square. Predrill screw holes through legs and into cross braces. Countersink holes to accept wooden plugs.

4. Disassemble end frames. Glue ends of all cross braces. Reassemble end frames on flat working surface, and insert screws. Tighten all screws firmly while checking for square and making sure upper cross brace is located flush with the top of and centered on the legs. Apply glue to wooden plugs; insert them into the holes and drive them in so they're nearly flush. When glue dries, trim excess plug and sand flush with leg. When both end frames are complete, turn them upside down.

5. Install top side rails by predrilling, gluing, and installing screws and wooden plugs as described in Steps 3 and 4. Be careful to provide enough clearance from previously installed screws on adjacent legs. Keep checking for square before glue sets so that screws can be backed off slightly to realign the unit and then tightened to hold it in correct position.

6. Install center bottom brace using the method described above while frame is still inverted.

❶

❷

❸

❹

❺

❺

Standard on
all joints

Not less
than 4" high

(Figure 1)

7. Turn table right side up and be sure alignment is correct and table sits squarely on flat surface.

8. Center sash on frame, making sure it is flush with frame. I chose to put the interior side of the sash up, but either side will work. Install screws through predrilled holes as shown through sash and into side rails of table. Apply glue to wooden plugs; insert them into holes and drive them in so they're nearly flush. When glue dries, trim excess plugs and sand flush with top.

9. Sand table lightly and prime. Let dry. Using a foam brush, paint two coats of black paint on table, allowing it to dry between each coat.

10. Trace stencil design twice (one for reverse image) on acetate and cut out with craft knife. Stencil design onto each side rail with gold stencil paint and stencil brush. **(Figure 2)**

(Figure 2)

Design Extra:
Put a piece of ¹/₄-inch glass cut to size on top of table to make a curio table. Put small treasures, interesting postcards, lace doilies, or pictures into each pane before covering with glass.

Wrap Pillow

A pillow adds detail and character to a sofa or chair, but a pillow with detail of its own adds an interesting focal point to the seat. A plain purchased pillow can be transformed into a decorative one with a splash of color from a scrap piece of fabric. The fabric is simply tied around the pillow and into a knot then fused in place.

Materials

Fabric
⅜-inch-wide roll of iron-on adhesive

1. To determine fabric yardage, measure pillow and add 2 inches to length. Multiply width by 2 ½.

2. Lay fabric right side down and fold both long edges 1 inch; press. Fuse edges with iron-on adhesive. Do not peel paper backing off adhesive. Center pillow in middle of fabric. Remove paper backing, turn pillow over, and press to fuse fabric to pillow. Bring ends of fabric to the front and tie into a neat knot. Tuck excess fabric into center of knot.

Design Extra:
Wrap a table runner or scarf around a pillow and secure with a decorative brooch or pin.

Any Season—Victorian

*A*t the turn of the century Victorian interiors were filled with dark woods, heavy fabrics, fringe, and lace adorning everything. Today's version of Victorian is much lighter but is still reminiscent of days gone by. The delicious mix of floral fabric, elegant damask, fine linens and lace, along with striped wallcoverings, give this room a feminine appeal. The sofa is contemporary but blends in beautifully when mixed with the right accessories. A Victorian room allows you to display your favorite things. If you have bookshelves, mix collectibles and books together. Place trinkets on top of a stack of books, put small mirrors in decorative frames to catch the light, and hang a beautiful piece of lace from one or more of the shelves. To vary the mix of collectibles, redecorate the room on occasion by shifting and moving things from one room or place to another. Put things away for a while, and when you bring them out again they will have a fresh, new appeal.

Throw Swags with Rosettes

(Figure 1)

Informal swags are one of the easiest window treatments to make. The finished look can be simple or elegant depending on how you drape (throw) them over swag holders or decorative rods. They can be used alone or combined with curtains, blinds, or a lace panel. Rosettes are easy to make and add a finishing touch to the window. Place the swags asymmetrically on the windows so the jabots fall to different lengths to create a different look. The draping is important to achieving the look you want. The swag pictured here was pulled down to bring the eye away from the very low ceiling in the room. The best fabrics to choose are light- to medium-weight fabrics like cotton chintz without a one-way design.

Materials

Fabric	Yardstick
String	2 swag holders (see page 70)
3/8-inch-wide roll of iron-on adhesive	Sewing gauge
	Pushpin

1. To determine fabric yardage, use entire width of fabric. For length, place a string over swag holders and drape across window; allow string to hang to desired length on each side of window; add 20 inches for each rosette; measure string for fabric yardage.

2. With wrong sides together, fold fabric in half lengthwise and press. On folded edge, measure 15 inches in from each corner and make a small pencil mark. Place a yardstick diagonally on fabric to connect pencil mark with outer corner of selvages. Draw a line. Repeat on other side. Cut fabric on marked lines. **(Figure 1)**

3. Open fabric and fold over all raw edges ½ inch, using a sewing gauge for accuracy; press. Fold fabric in half again, making sure folded edges meet all around. Fuse with iron-on adhesive along fabric edges. **(Figure 2)**

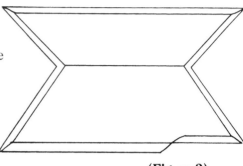

(Figure 2)

4. Hang fabric over swag holders so the center of the fabric is placed exactly over the center of the window. Use a pushpin to hold in place temporarily. **(Figure 3)**

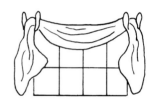

(Figure 3)

5. Create a loop by drawing up 20 inches of fabric from the length of fabric hanging below the swag holder. Place the loop into the U-shaped grip so that it hangs over the front of the grip. **(Figure 4)**

6. Form a half-open fan by pulling the fabric edges out of the fan. Squeeze the U-shaped grip together to lock fabric in place. **(Figure 5)**

(Figure 4)

7. Make a rosette by spreading out the fabric of the loop. Bring the two ends together and tuck one open end into the other. **(Figure 6)**

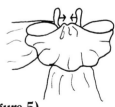

(Figure 5)

Design Extra:

Create perfect folds in a swag. Before hanging swag in holders, accordion-fold entire length of fabric and use clothespins about every 12 inches to hold folds in place until you get the swag up onto the swag holders. Remove clothespins and gently arrange folds.

(Figure 6)

Tablecloth Curtain

Lace is a beautiful accent for the perfect Victorian look but may be very costly to purchase by the yard. I have found that lace tablecloths are ideal to use as curtain panels because all the edges are finished and they look as splendid as European lace while costing very little. The length of your window will determine the size of the tablecloth you should purchase. Allow extra for header, rod pocket, and hem. I used iron-on adhesive to make the panels pictured here. Most manufacturers recommend testing the iron-on adhesive on lace first.

Materials

1 lace tablecloth
Sewing gauge

⅜-inch-wide roll of iron-on adhesive

1. Measure length of window, adding 9 inches for header and rod pocket (conventional 1-inch-wide rod). If necessary, cut tablecloth to length at one end.
2. Using a sewing gauge, measure ¼ inch from cut edge and fold over. Fold over again 4 inches and press. Open second fold and measure 2 inches down from fold line for placement of top line of iron-on adhesive. Place other strip of adhesive right on ¼-inch fold. Fuse iron-on adhesive and remove paper backing. Fold fabric back over onto adhesive, matching corners, and press. Let cool. **(Figure 1)**
3. Push rod through rod pocket and hang.

Design Extra:
Fold an extra-long oblong tablecloth in half widthwise. Place over curtain rod so short ends meet. Bring half of the cloth to one side of window and tie back with decorative ribbon. Attach to the wall with thumbtack. Repeat on other half, but bring to opposite side of window to create a quick window treatment.

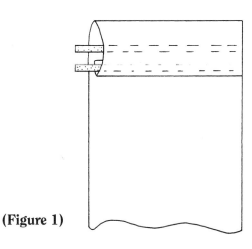

(Figure 1)

Coat-Hanger Swag Holder

(Figure 1)

(Figure 2)

(Figure 3)

(Figure 4)

(Figure 5)

(Figure 6)

(Figure 7)

(Figure 8)

Many different types of swag holders are available to hang swag valances. If you have more than one window treatment to make, a simple treatment can become expensive because of the hardware involved. By using wire coat hangers you can create your own for free. This allows you to spend more money where it counts—on beautiful fabric. You can drape a swag through the holder, tie knots, or make rosettes.

Materials

Wire clothes hanger (Use a medium- or heavy-weight hanger for best results)

Needle-nose pliers
Wire cutters

1. Open hanger with pliers at twisted section. **(Figure 1)**
2. Using pliers, bend twisted section down onto shoulder part of hanger. **(Figure 2)**
3. To make projection, form an L shape, then a 3-inch projection (approximate). Make the projection longer or shorter depending on the window and what kind of treatment is underneath. **(Figure 3)**
4. Make another L-shaped curve and go up approximately 3 inches to start the U-shaped part of the swag holder. Keep molding hanger to form U. **(Figure 4)**
5. Next, make another projection to go back, parallel with the other. **(Figure 5)**
6. Bend hanger to form base section to look like the opposite side. **(Figure 6)**
7. Cut excess hanger at projection base using wire cutters. **(Figure 7)**
8. Pinch wire together where nails go. Mount swag holder in the upper corners of window or on the wall 2 inches diagonally up from corner of window frame. **(Figure 8)**

Quick Topiary

Topiaries give green plants character as well as a hint of elegance and are fun to grow. I love the way a topiary looks placed by a chair, door, or on a mantel, but I have a brown thumb and little time to care for plants. That's why I decided to make a topiary from silk ivy. Experiment with different shapes and sizes of plastic foam to make unique topiaries of all sizes. For instance, a small ball on top of a cone shape makes an interesting shape. When purchasing silk ivy, choose ivy with small leaves.

Materials

Plastic foam for pot
Clay pot
Long, thin, flexible twigs to wrap around stem
Straight tree branch about ½ inch in diameter, cut into three 7-inch sections
4-, 5-, and 6-inch plastic foam balls
Spanish moss
Paper clips or florist's pins
4 long silk ivy vines with small leaves
Hot-glue gun and glue sticks

1. Put a block of plastic foam into a clay pot. Wrap a thin branch around each straight branch to resemble a vine growing up the stem. Push one 7-inch stick into the 4-inch ball and the other end of the stick into the 5-inch ball. Push another stick into bottom of 5-inch ball and top of 6-inch ball. Push the last stick into bottom of 6-inch ball and the other end into center of foam in clay pot.
2. Cover each ball with Spanish moss. Use florist's pins or open up paper clips and fold them in half. Push into balls to hold moss in place. Place some moss in base of pot to hide plastic foam.
3. Cut some ivy leaves off vine at base of stems. Hot-glue leaves to moss. Wind some intact vines around each ball and use pins to hold in place. To fill out foliage, cut off a few clumps of leaves and hot-glue in bunches around each ball. Cover each ball as much as you like. Leave some vines intact to spill out from top of clay pot.

Design Extra:
Accent stem of topiary by tying a bow with French ribbon or colored raffia.

Picture Bow and Ribbon

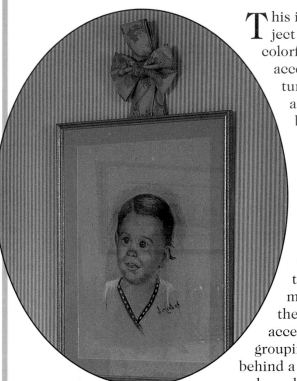

This is a quick project that adds a colorful and elegant accent to a picture hanging on a wall. Picture bows and streamers were originally used to hide the wire when pictures were suspended on wire attached to ceiling molding. Try the bows to accent picture groupings, hung behind a mirror, or even draped over the frame of a door that has no decorative molding to create interest. Make streamers as long or as short as you need. The finished streamers pictured here are 26 inches long. Use moiré for an elegant look or let the picture in the frame dictate what type of fabric you should use.

Materials

1 ¼ yards fabric
Fabric glue

5-inch florist's wire

1. Lay fabric right side up and cut 4 strips:
   two 8 x 45-inch pieces for streamers
   one 10 x 13-inch piece for knot
   one 13 x 18-inch piece for loop
2. On each streamer piece, fold one long edge under ¼-inch and press. Then fold both long edges to center, overlapping slightly, with raw edge under folded edge. Press. Run a line of fabric glue right under overlap to adhere edges together and press. **(Figure 1)**
3. Lay each streamer face up and tuck one end up inside to create a diagonal end. Repeat with other streamer, making sure point is reversed. Press. Run a line of glue just inside edges and press. **(Figure 2)**
4. To assemble, lay streamers face up one on top of the other, making sure diagonal ends point out. Fold top edges of streamers down to the back 5 inches. **(Figure 3)**
5. To make knot, fold 13-inch sides into center, slightly overlapping, and press.
6. For loops, fold 18-inch sides into center of strip, overlapping slightly. Do not press. Fold short ends into center, overlapping edges about 1 inch.
7. Lay knot strip vertically on table, overlapped edges face up. Place loop section, overlapped edges face up horizontally, on knot strip and tie knot strip around loop piece. **(Figure 4)**
8. Turn to front and pinch front of knot and primp bow loops. Place loop and knot 5 inches below fold on streamers, using excess from knot piece to tie loops tightly onto streamers. Double-knot and cut or tuck excess knot piece into the back of knot. **(Figure 5)**
9. To make hanger, fold 5-inch piece of wire in half and twist, leaving a loop to go over a nail on the wall. Thread behind knot on back of bow so that wire loop is on top of knot. Bring twisted ends up to twist back onto the wire. Hang behind picture, separating the streamers behind the picture. **(Figure 6)**

Design Extra:
To make one wide streamer for bow, cut only one 45-inch strip, but widen to 10 inches.

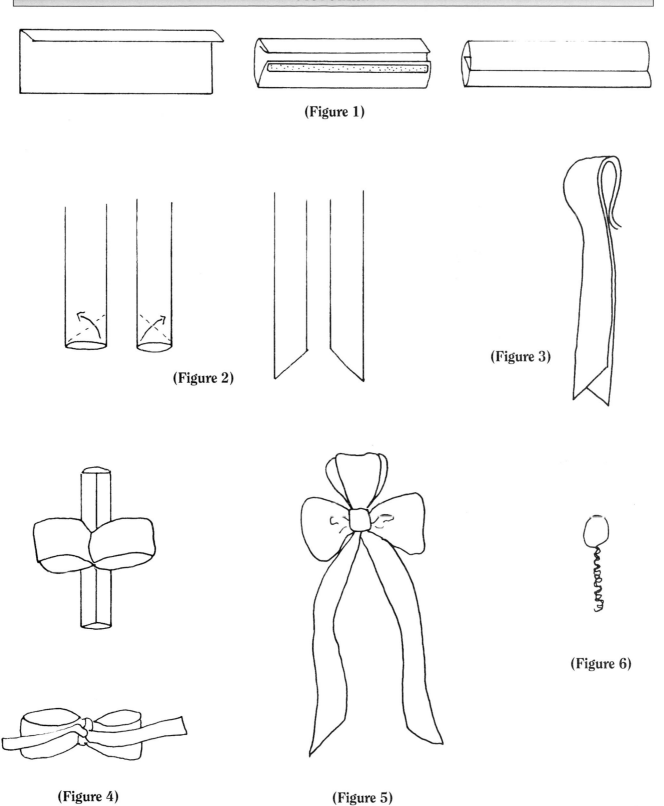

(Figure 1)

(Figure 2)

(Figure 3)

(Figure 4)

(Figure 5)

(Figure 6)

CHAPTER THREE

DINING ROOMS

A formal dining room is usually the least used room in the house. With the exception of special occasions, a visual rope seems to be placed across the door that says "Keep out and don't touch!" Rather than just going in to dust, learn to enjoy the room and use it frequently to savor the pleasure of its purpose. When you decorate, express your personality and tell a story about your lifestyle and the way you like to entertain. A successfully decorated dining room may be a cozy round table for four, crystal chandeliers, dramatic window or wall treatments, or a room with ceiling beams, an open-shelved hutch, and a large rectangular pine table with benches to seat the entire family, including the grandchildren. Add details to the room that reflect your personal style, a favorite collection, or family memorabilia, treasures, and photos. The things you love will give the space its character and essence. It will be filled with pleasant memories—a place you'll want to use frequently.

Formal Dining Room

*T*o heighten the drama of a traditional dining room, decorate with colors in deep jewel tones to create an elegant ambiance. Chairs take on added importance when placed against deep-colored walls, creating a balance between the cream-colored carpet and the lighter walls. Accent framed art by centering a stencil above the frame and stenciling in gold. Placing a decorative wallpaper border in a coordinating scheme, making a chandelier cover, and using ruched cord on the window treatment add the finishing touches that make the room a more gracious place.

Bishop's Sleeves with Ruched Cord

*B*ishop's sleeves are big poufs draped into the fabric that fall vertically from the rod. They add mid-length detail to any curtain panel and are a lovely way to formally dress a window without blocking the light. The jewel-tone fabric presents a dramatic contrast to the light-colored walls. The rod is covered with a tube of shirred fabric with a heading. Hung between the panels are purchased lace balloon shades that give the entire window a finished look while still allowing light to filter through. Bishop's sleeves can be made on any curtain panel. If you purchase panels for bishop's sleeves, make sure they are extra-long to allow for poufs. Bishop's sleeves look especially elegant when the fabric puddles on the floor.

Materials

Fabric	1 ½ yards of ½-inch cord
⅜-inch-wide roll of iron-on adhesive	24 inches of ½-inch-wide ribbon, cut in half
Coordinating fabric for cord tieback	Pushpins
	Safety pins

1. To determine fabric yardage for each panel, add 20 inches to the rod-to-floor measurement for length. Use the entire width of fabric for panel width. To measure for shirred rod cover, measure length of curtain rod between two panels and multiply by 2 for length; width of rod plus 4 ½ inches is width heading. For coordinating cord tieback, use a strip 3 inches wide and 108 inches (3 yards) long.

2. Cut fabric panel to size. Fuse all sides with iron-on adhesive to make finished edges. Lay fabric right side down. Fold top edge over ¼ inch and press. Fold over again 2 inches, plus width of rod. Press. Open fold and place two lines of ⅜-inch iron-on adhesive as shown. Bottom strip of adhesive should be placed over first fold (¼ inch) edge. Rod should slip through space, leaving a 2-inch heading on curtain panel. Press and remove paper backing from adhesive. Lay folded section back over fabric, lining up corner edges of fabric. Press. Let cool. **(Figure 1)**

3. For shirred rod cover, lay fabric strip right side down. Fold long sides over ¼ inch and press. Fold strip in half lengthwise, matching folded edges; press. Place a ⅜-inch strip of iron-on adhesive 2 inches below top edges and press to fuse. Put another strip of iron-on adhesive along top edge and press to fuse. **(Figure 2)**

4. Cover the ½-inch cord for tiebacks using coordinating fabric. (See page 14.)

5. Hang one panel on rod and gather to one side. Put rod cover on next, then second panel.

6. To make poufs in panels, tie 12-inch-long ribbon around panel ½ to ¾ below top of window. Bring ribbon behind panel and pull up about 6 inches. Knot ribbon. Use pushpin to attach to wall or window molding. Pull up fabric and then let it rest over the ribbon, hiding it. Fan out panel above tied ribbon to make pouf.

7. Wrap covered cord tieback two times around panel below pouf. Safety-pin ends together in back of panel. Arrange cord and let hang in front of pouf in fabric.

(Figure 1)

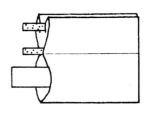

(Figure 2)

Knotted Chair-Back Slips

Dining-room furniture takes little abuse and is usually replaced far less frequently than other furniture in a home. To perk up a look that has remained the same throughout the years, modify the color scheme with paint, wallpaper, and accessories. Instead of emphasizing the center of the table, occasionally make different pieces of furniture more prominent using fabric and color accents such as with slipcovers on the chairs. Matched with coordinated seat covers, back slips give the impression of upholstered chairs, yet are easier to take care of because they can be removed for cleaning. Make your own pattern by tracing the outlines of your chair directly on the fabric. If knots are too formal, make bows with coordinating fabric or leave the back plain.

Materials

Fabric
⅜-inch-wide roll of iron-on adhesive

Pins
Pencil

1. To determine fabric yardage for each slipcover, measure for length by measuring height of chair back from bottom of seat to top and adding 2 inches. For width, measure around the chair, adding 3 inches. For width of knotted tieback, measure across width of chair back at widest part and add 10 inches. Length of tieback is 13 inches. Cut fabric for tieback according to measurements.

2. Fold fabric for slipcover right sides together and lay on floor. Place chair back on fabric and trace with pencil. From traced line measure 1 ½ inches for seam allowance, plus the depth of chair back. Mark that measurement from traced line and draw a new line. Cut on outside line. **(Figure 1)**

3. Lay tieback strip right side down. Fold edges into center, overlapping slightly. Fuse edges together with iron-on adhesive. Tie loose knot in middle of strip. Arrange knot so seam doesn't show.

4. Lay fabric for back of chair right side up. Center knotted strip on fabric and pin ends to back piece. Trim excess if necessary. Put front piece right side down and align top and side edges. Pin all thicknesses together. From just below knotted strip sew on pencil line.

5. Turn fabric to right side. Fuse or sew a hem on sides and bottom edges of cover.

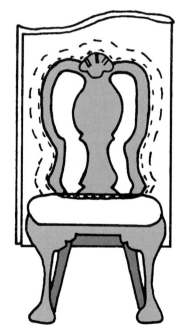

(Figure 1)

Design Extra:
Hot-glue ruched or coordinating color cord around chair on top of seam.

Chandelier Chain Cover

For a hint of surprise and a dash of color in an unexpected place, cover your chandelier chain with fabric. Chandelier chain covers are available through home-furnishing catalogs, but why spend money on details that you can easily make using scraps from coordinating fabric. Using this method to cover a chain does not require removal of the fixture from the ceiling.

Materials

Fabric
⅜-inch-wide iron-on adhesive
    or fabric glue
Matching thread

Sewing needle
Sticky back hook and loop
    fastener, cut to the length
    of chain

1. Cut fabric into a long strip two times the length of chain; width is 4 inches. Lay fabric right side down. Fold all edges over ½ inch and fuse to make finished edges with iron-on adhesive or fabric glue.

2. Knot the end of a piece of thread as long as chain. Sew a running stitch along one long edge of fabric strip. Leave thread on needle and unknotted. Repeat on other long edge. **(Figure 1)**

3. Gather fabric on threads until fabric is the length of chain. Secure thread on each side by taking a few stitches on edge of fabric and knotting end. Cut excess thread. **(Figure 2)**

4. Lay gathered strip right side up. Put hook of hook and loop fastener ⅛ inch away from left outside edge. Turn fabric over so right side of fabric is down and place loop ¼ inch from left inside edge. Press all edges of hook and loop fastener to fabric for proper adhesion. **(Figure 3)**

5. Stand on ladder and wrap cover around chain. Attach hook to loop of fastener to cover chain.

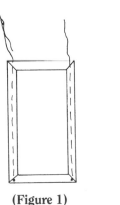

(Figure 1)

(Figure 2)

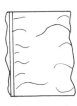

(Figure 3)

CHAPTER FOUR

BEDROOMS

A bedroom should be a warm and inviting haven away from the daily grind of a busy world. It is your private sanctuary. Give the bed more style and importance by placing two to four large pillows to coordinate with the bed cover. The rest of the room can be planned around this focal point. Instead of decorating the bedroom with a perfectly matched set of furniture, make it more interesting with a variety of textures and shapes. Try mixing furniture styles and pieces to relax the space, making the room feel more comfortable. Choose warm and calming colors to further heighten the sense of comfort. Use more intimate lighting in a bedroom. Small table lamps with soft white or pink bulbs with sufficient wattage for reading placed on both sides of the bed will truly make the bedroom a relaxing retreat.

Floral Bedroom

When choosing colors for a bedroom, select those that are soothing to you and make you feel relaxed. Pink, though a feminine color, has been proven to be a very relaxing color for men, too. Matching fabrics, paint, and wallcoverings can be difficult at times, and most of us tend to be timid when we are faced with too many choices of colors and patterns. Forget the word match and think coordination. Use three or four coordinating fabrics and add different textures and accents. It's especially easy when the fabrics are pre-selected by the manufacturer and grouped in a collection of colors and prints. This bedroom has white walls and trim. The windows and bed share an awning stripe with a floral-and-vine design that adds a beautiful contrast. A shiny pink tassel and cutwork lace provide the needed texture to give the room a visually stimulating look. Pile the bed with pillows and snuggle in. The shade cover on the bedside lamp is accented with crinkle ribbon for a unique touch. The larger lamp is covered with fabric to conceal a big hole in the base; decorative cord holds the fabric in place.

Window-Molding Decoupage

*M*ost window treatments cover the window and leave the molding exposed. If the molding or wall above your window is plain, give it a burst of color to further unify the window treatment. I cut the flowers from fabric scraps left from pillows I had made. If you are using a fabric pattern that has a few different designs on it, mix the designs across the molding. When placing designs, try to arrange them so they appear to be in motion. With a geometric pattern, a straight arrangement would be more appropriate. To save time, I always do the mindless parts of a project that don't require intense concentration, like cutting designs from fabric or paper, while I watch television or listen to the radio.

cardboard. Starting from the center of your sketch, place your cutout designs in different ways until you find a placement you like.

3. Make sure molding is clean and free of dust. Start with center cutout and brush decoupage medium on the back using foam paintbrush. Once piece has been positioned on molding, brush a coat of decoupage medium on top of it. Repeat this procedure for each piece, ensuring that all air bubbles are brushed out. Brush a top coat of decoupage medium over entire area and let dry.

Materials

Patterned fabric

Paper or cardboard

Decoupage medium

Foam paintbrush

1. Cut out designs from fabric.
2. Measure width and length of top portion of window molding and sketch the dimensions on a sheet of paper or

Design Extra:

Before finishing any decorating project, ask yourself, "What can I do to make this uniquely mine?" or "What special touch could I add to this?" I stenciled a swaged floral garland along the top of the walls in my room and accented it by adding satin ribbon bows to each peak in the garland. This gave a purchased stencil a three-dimensional look and made it uniquely mine.

No-Sew Balloon Shades

The balloon shade on this window is stationary, but the inexpensive roller shade behind it moves to provide privacy or light when I want it. The crisp awning-stripe fabric coordinates with the loosely- rendered overall rose pattern and garden-theme vine design on the comforter and bench skirt. Balloon shades add softness and depth to small or uninteresting windows. The poufs can be made to go straight across, dip down slightly, or up in the middle. Finials on standard cafe-style rods are usually very small. I removed the existing small ones with pliers and replaced them with larger wooden ones spray-painted gold.

Materials

Fabric

⅝-inch-wide-roll of iron-on adhesive or fabric glue

Pencil

Skein of matching embroidery floss

Large-eyed needle

1. To determine fabric yardage, measure length of window from top of rod to sill and add 12 inches for length. Measure width of window from inside of frame to inside of frame; multiply by 2 ½ for fabric width.

2. Using iron-on adhesive, fuse a finished edge to all sides of fabric.

3. Lay fabric right side down and fold top edge over the width of rod plus 1 ½ inches and press. Open fold and place a strip of iron-on adhesive or fabric glue along top edge. Fuse and press to make a rod pocket without a heading.

4. Lay fabric right side up on large work surface or floor. Using a pencil, make a small mark on bottom corner on each side of shade.

5. Measure the distance between the two marks. Divide that measurement into the number of poufs you want across the bottom of the shade. (There are six small poufs on this shade. If you prefer larger poufs, make three or four.) Then mark that measurement across the bottom edge with a pencil.

6. Hang fabric on rod and place on window. Thread about 18 inches of floss onto a needle and knot end. Starting at center mark, sew 2 inch running stitches vertically from pencil mark to the level poufs are to fall. Push fabric up on floss to gather for poufs. Bring needle and floss to back of fabric and tie floss tightly to knotted end. Trim excess floss. Repeat for each mark. **(Figure 1)**

7. Arrange poufs by pushing your fist behind each pouf to gently spread fabric out.

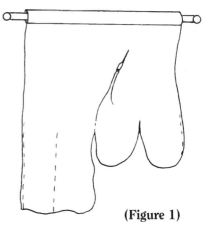

(Figure 1)

Design Extra:
Make pillow shams for a bed or cover a lamp base with fabric that coordinates with one element on the windows. This will visually balance the colors throughout a room.

Tablecloth Valance with Tassel

*B*attenburg lace is an excellent choice for comple-menting a floral motif. There are two windows in this room; to save money, I cut one square lace table-cloth in half diagonally to cover both windows. If you have only one window, drape the entire cloth over the rod so that the cloth can still be used for its original purpose later. If your windows are very wide, place a few cloths across the window, creating several points instead of just one. Adding a tassel accented with a gold bead gives the valance a distinct decorator touch.

Materials

One 42-inch square Batten-
   burg lace tablecloth
Tassel (see page 29)
1 gold bead

8 skeins of embroidery floss
   to coordinate with room
   decor

1. Press tablecloth. Drape diagonally over rod and existing balloon shade, centering point.
2. Make tassel (see page 29). Slip gold bead through two top strands on tassel. Tie tassel onto tablecloth at center point through a hole in the lace. Trim excess strands of floss.

Design Extra:
Why keep all of your beautiful possessions hidden? Take the lace tablecloth you never use for fear of staining it, for example. Think how marvelous it would look tucked between your sheets and comforter, folded over to create a beautiful lace edge for the top and sides of the comforter.

Piano-Bench Skirt

A bench placed at the end of a bed adds a special quality to the room, making it more than just a place to sleep in—it's also a retreat. Use the bench to sit on when changing your clothes, as a table for stacking a pile of books, or to hold a tray for a soothing nightcap in bed. I resurrected an old piano bench from the attic to use as my bedroom bench; if I had not looked beyond its "piano" use, it would still be collecting dust in the attic. Instead of refinishing, I covered it with coordinating fabrics to add color to the room. The fabric is stapled on, and hems are fused with iron-on adhesive. If you have a bench with elegantly carved legs in good shape, make a shorter skirt or just cover the top.

Materials

Fabric
2-inch-thick foam cut to
    size of bench top
Staple gun and staples
Hot-glue gun and glue
    sticks
⅜-inch-wide roll of adhesive
    or iron-on fabric glue

1. To determine fabric yardage for seat, measure length and width, adding 10 inches to each measurement. For knotted band, measure around bench and add 15 inches for length; width is 12 inches. For skirt, measure around bench and multiply by 2 for fabric length; measure from floor to just below bench seat and add 1 inch for fabric width.

2. If bench opens, remove screws and take seat off. Hot-glue foam to seat top.

3. Lay fabric for seat right side down. Center seat on fabric, foam side down. Wrap fabric around the seat and staple to back of seat. Staple the two long sides first, then the short sides. To make smooth corners, pull fabric at corner and work into small pleats to eliminate bulk. Staple to secure and trim excess.

4. Lay skirt fabric right side down. Fold fabric ¼ inch along bottom edge and sides; press. Fold over again ½ inch and fuse with iron-on adhesive or fabric glue and press.

5. Fold fabric in half so short edges meet. Staple top of fabric at center fold to front center of bench, along inside top edge of open bench. Make a 1-inch-wide pleat and staple. Working to the right, continue by making pleats about 1½ inches apart and stapling. Continue to the center back of bench, then begin again at center front and work to the left until you reach the center back. Overlap fabric edges and staple. Trim excess fabric from top edge.

6. Lay fabric for knotted band right side down. Fold both long edges to center, overlapping slightly. Tie a loose knot in the center of fabric, making sure edges do not show on right side. Center knot in front of bench and staple to top inside edge over skirt. Pull and staple fabric taut around corners. Staple ends in back along top edge. Arrange fold in knotted band with fingers. Replace seat.

Design Extra:

Move the bench around the room occasionally. Placing it in front of a window gives you a window seat and it anchors the window treatment.

Lace-Edged Napkin Pillow

*P*illows in all shapes, sizes, and patterns look marvelous practically everywhere. Delicate lace used to accent a pillow in a floral bedroom provides the perfect finishing touch. If you have an old pillow that no longer fits in with your decor, simply cover it by weaving ribbon through the crocheted edges of two napkins. Look for decorative trim on napkins and add colorful ribbons to make a pillow truly special for a bedroom.

Materials

Two 18-inch square napkins
 with crocheted edges
15-inch square pillow or form

2 yards of 1-inch-wide ribbon
Large-eyed needle

1. Press napkins. Center pillow on one napkin. Place second napkin on top, matching corners. Thread ribbon through needle. Starting from one corner, weave ribbon around pillow through the open pattern of crocheted edges, weaving over a few "holes" each time. Tie excess ribbon into a knot and tuck in or make a decorative bow.

Ruched Cord and Bow Pillow

*A*dd comfort to a wooden bench or window seat by placing decorative pillows on it. This pillow, as purchased, had the green-bow print on a white ground. I found fabric with an all-over green splatter design to coordinate, then used it to cover a cord and hot-glued it around the pillow's edge. The bow was made by folding fabric strips and tying them together.

Materials

Coordinating fabric for cord
 cover and bow
Purchased pillow
½-inch cord, circumference of
 pillow plus 2 inches

Hot-glue gun and glue sticks
Needle and thread
Fabric glue
Fabric stiffener or white glue
 diluted with water

1. Measure fabric for cord cover and bow. For cord cover, measure the circumference of the pillow and multiply by 2 for the length; use 4 inches for width. Top loop of bow measures 4 x 11 inches; bottom loop of bow is 4 x 14 inches; tail is 4 x 13 inches; knot is 4 x 7 inches. Cut fabric to sizes measured.
2. Cover and ruche fabric on cord following directions on page 14.
3. Starting from top right-hand corner of pillow, place a line of hot glue on one side of pillow on seam. Press seam side of cord into hot glue. Continue around pillow until ends of cord meet. Sew a few stitches to hold cord ends together.
4. Lay fabric strips for bow right side down and fold long edges to middle, overlapping slightly; press. Use fabric glue to adhere edges on each strip.
5. Lay bottom loop seam side up and fold short edges to middle. Turn to right side. Repeat for top loop. Place top loop on bottom loop. Find center of tail piece and pinch. Center pinched area under center of loops. Lay knot piece vertically on center of loops and tie tightly around all three pieces. Double-knot in back and trim excess. Brush fabric stiffener on tail ends to prevent fraying. When stiffener dries, cut ends of tails in a V or diagonal cut. Hot-glue bow to corner of pillow where ruched cord meets.

Pearl Picture Frame

*T*he materials used for this unusual frame came from old junk. An old picture frame that had lost its luster, imitation pearls found at a flea market years ago, and hot glue are all I needed. I was inspired to make this after I saw something similar at a store for an exorbitant price. The choice of beads used will determine its style. Try colored plastic beads for a child's frame, crystal beads for an elegant frame, or wooden beads for a country frame. Each frame takes only 20 minutes to assemble and makes a great bridal gift or surprise for family and friends.

Materials

2 ½ x 3 ½-inch frame
Hot-glue gun and glue sticks
10-15 small gold beads

18 inches or longer imitation pearl necklace or 2 shorter ones

1. Remove glass and back from frame.

2. Put a thick line of hot glue on one side of frame. Lay one opened end of necklace on hot glue. Press gently. Continue gluing necklace onto front of frame, then to side of frame. If second necklace is needed, start where first one ends.

3. After frame has been covered, start overlapping necklace by putting the hot glue on top of the first layer of pearls until desired thickness is achieved. Make sure clasps of necklace are covered. Trim excess.

4. In random spots, hot-glue small gold beads to frame for accents. Reassemble frame.

Design Extra:
To coordinate your bedroom with pillows and fabrics, refer to page 25 for instructions to make a fabric-covered lamp base and to page 41 for a shirred lampshade.

Rainbow Palette Girl's Room

A child's room should be a fun, bright, and whimsical place. It should not be just a room for sleeping but also a learning center where discovery and creative play occur. If you have enough space, add a table and chairs to the room so the children can sit and draw or play. Add shelves so they can have their toys and crayons nearby. To make children feel really comfortable, let them help decorate. To make everybody happy, make up a list of colors and ideas you like and have your child pick from your list. As long as the room remains functional, respect the choices on where things should be placed even if you would prefer to have it another way. If your child makes the bed but doesn't place the pillows just right, resist the urge to fix it. Instead, learn to enjoy and watch the youngster's growing sense of aesthetics. This will encourage self-confidence and trust.

Clothespin Bow Valance

A long, rectangular piece of fabric is the most versatile shape for a window valance. It can be draped, knotted, or twisted over a rod on a window of any size to create different effects. It is a perfect decorating treatment for apartments or college dormitories because it goes up easily and can be changed dramatically to fit different-size windows. A valance adds color and style while requiring only a small amount of fabric, which minimizes the cost. The clothespins are holding up this charming valance and are clipped to the existing balloon-shade rod. With the eye-catching bows, the valance takes on the personality of the little girl who occupies the room. Weave different colors of ribbon through the lace trim of purchased balloon shades to tie them into the color scheme.

Materials

Fabric

Coordinating fabric for lining

Small bottle of paint, same color as fabric

2 or more spring-type clothespins

⅜-inch-wide roll of iron-on adhesive or fabric glue

Hot-glue gun and glue sticks

Cafe rod

1. Directions are for a single window. To determine fabric yardage for valance, measure width of the window from outside edge of trim to outside edge of trim; multiply by 2½ and use this amount for length. Width of fabric is 17 inches. For each bow, measure 10 x 36-inch fabric strips.

2. Paint clothespins and let dry.
3. Cut valance fabric and lining to size. On each piece, fold all edges to wrong side ½ inch and press. Lay wrong sides together, matching up all edges. Fuse the two pieces together along the folded edges with iron-on adhesive or fabric glue.
4. On each strip of bow fabric, fold all sides under ¼ inch and press. Fold each piece in half lengthwise matching corners and edges. Fuse edges together, press.
5. Form one finished strip of bow fabric into a loose M-shape and tie one loop (hump of M) over the other, as if you were tying your shoes. Adjust bow loops and straighten out knot. **(Figure 1)** Center bow on clothespin and hot-glue on one side of clothespin. **(Figure 2)**
6. Clip clothespins on rod where desired. Center valance on rod and drape each side behind a clothespin. Pull center fabric down to drape. Pull fabric from behind clothespins to drape in front. Lift rod from its bracket and tuck a small part of the top edge of valance over the rod and back into the bracket to hold fabric on sides, allowing about 10 inches to drape down each side of the window without the use of another clothespin. Make sure valance is draped evenly.

(Figure 1)   **(Figure 2)**

Design Extra:
Instead of gluing bows to the clothespins, try shells, pinecones, decorative coasters, craft cutouts, or sponge shapes. For a boy's room, glue a baseball card to each clothespin and glue the cards on at a different angle across the top of the valance to suggest motion or activity.

Sponge-Stamped Walls

Let the kids help decorate the room with this fun project. It is quick, easy, and very inexpensive to do. The shapes are cut from sponges, dipped in paint, and stamped on the walls. My daughter and I used five different shapes and colors, and concentrated the placement of the shapes on the center of each wall. Make your own shapes from sponges by drawing a design on them with a marking pen and cutting out. We used leftover foam carpet padding, which produces less texture than a sponge. If you prefer, look in crafts shops for sponges in all shapes and sizes.

Materials

Cellulose sponges
Felt-tipped marker
Scissors
Blocks of wood or plastic
   foam to attach sponge
   shapes for stamping

Hot-glue gun and glue
   sticks
2-ounce acrylic paints in
   desired colors
Pie tins, enough for each
   color paint

1. Draw shapes on sponges with marker and cut out with scissors. If you prefer, trace the bottom of cans and small boxes. Cut a square out of plastic foam or wood a little larger than sponge shape. Center and hot-glue sponge shape to block.
2. Pour one color of paint into each pie tin and designate a color for each shape.
3. Start with one shape at a time. Hold block and press sponge into paint in pie tin, being sure to cover sponge. Blot gently on paper towel. Stamp shape on the wall in a random pattern. After two or three stamps, you will need more paint. Remember to leave plenty of space for other colors and shapes. Continue around room. Then add a second color and shape. After all the shapes have been stamped on wall, step back to see if any areas could use a few more shapes for color and balance.

Design Extra:
Make a radiator cover look like a cozy window seat by covering a piece of foam with fabric. Secure the underside with safety pins and place on top of radiator. Use hook and loop fastener to attach the skirt.

Fabric-Padded Headboard

No sewing or upholstery experience is needed to make a beautiful headboard for a bed. The trick to making it easier is having the plywood cut at the lumberyard and having no legs to attach. This headboard is attached to the wall above the bed. Padded headboards add color and texture and break up the uniform look of a perfectly matched set of bedroom furniture. A padded headboard makes the bed look very inviting and is comfortable to lean against when reading in bed. Instead of covering the border of the headboard with one piece of fabric, I covered it with four different striped fabrics. Each fabric was cut into pieces, then pleated and stapled to the headboard consecutively to achieve a rainbow effect. Decorative cord is used to hide the staples between the center and border fabrics. A quick way to finish the headboard is to buy cord that coordinates with your fabric. I could not find any in purple so I made a ruched cord cover to hide a plain white cord.

Materials

Fabric for center of headboard
Coordinating fabric for border cut into fifteen 10 x 10-inch pieces for a twin bed
¼- or ½-inch plywood, cut to bed size
Pencil
1-inch foam, cut 10 inches larger than bed size
Hot-glue gun and glue sticks

Rolled quilt batting
Staple gun and staples
Felt-tipped marker
Twisted paper cord
½- to 1-inch diameter decorative cord
Coordinating fabric to cover cord, if necessary
1-3 saw-toothed picture hangers, depending on bed size

Design Extra:
Make a pillow from two round doilies, stuff with batting, and weave colorful ribbons through the lace edge to close. Tie ends of ribbons into a bow.

Approximate Sizes:

	Twin	Full	Queen	King
Standard Bed Size	24" x 39"	24" x 54"	24" x 61"	24" x 76"
Center fabric	1 yard	1-2 yards	2-3 yards	2-3 yards
Border fabric	1 yard	1 ½ yards	2-3 yards	2-3 yards
2-inch foam	34" x 49"	34" x 64"	34" x 71"	34" x 86"
Quilt batting	34" x 49"	34" x 64"	34" x 71"	34" x 86"
Twisted paper cord	2 ½ yards	2 ¾ yards	3 yards	3 ½ yards
Decorative cord	2 ½ yards	2 ¾ yards	3 yards	3 ½ yards

1. To determine measurements for fabric and materials, see above.
2. Trace headboard pattern and either enlarge on a photocopier or draw your own. Make one copy, then turn traced pattern over on copier. Make second copy for reverse image for opposite side of headboard. **(Figure 1)**
3. Transfer pattern to plywood by drawing over the photocopy with a pencil. Turn copy over and rub with pencil point over wrong side of copy. Graphite from pencil will leave the pattern on the plywood. Use second copy to draw other half of headboard on plywood. Cut plywood along pattern lines.
4. Center and hot-glue foam to plywood. Lay batting on work surface and center headboard face down on quilt batting. Bring edges of batting and foam to back and staple taut on all sides.
5. Turn headboard to right side. Mark with felt-tipped pen from outside edge 5 inches around sides and top for border. Untwist paper cord no wider than ½ inch. Starting from bottom left, lay cord over drawn line and place vertical staples about every inch along cord into plywood around headboard. This will make a groove in the foam.

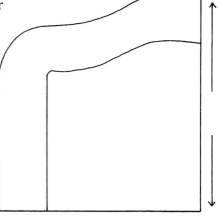

(Figure 1)

6. Cut center piece of fabric to fit slightly over cord. Staple fabric along paper cord, then bring bottom to back and staple taut.

7. Cut fabric for border pieces into 10 x 10-inch pieces. The number of pieces needed will be determined by the size of each pleat and the size of the headboard. Lay first piece at center top, fold a pleat in fabric, and staple edge to cord. Continue pleating and stapling fabric. Turn side edges of fabric under before stapling each piece. Add consecutive colors in one direction until you reach the bottom. Loosely pleat top of each piece and staple taut to back of headboard. Repeat from center to opposite side. Your paper cord is now covered with fabric and staples.

8. If you are going to make a ruched cord cover you will need a strip of fabric that is 3 inches wide and double the width of the bed. This fabric can be pieced by fusing fabric together to make one long piece. When the fabric is ruched the seams are hidden. To make a ruched cord cover to hide plain cord, see page 14.

9. Place a line of hot glue over staples and press decorative or ruched cord into groove to hide staples. Staple ends of cord to the back of headboard.

10. Attach 2 large pieces of picture-hanging hardware to each side on back of headboard. Place a third in the center for a queen- or king-size bed. Center right above bed and hang.

Painted Plaid and Lace Night Table

*F*lea-market finds, neighbors' castoffs, and forgotten attic treasures can all be given a new and exciting life with paint. Paint can transform anything. A piece that is painted is one of a kind and will add a unique and interesting accent to a room. Decorating a child's room with painted furniture will add the color, excitement, and whimsy that will make the room especially appealing. If you have a roomful of unmatched furniture, paint each piece in the same or coordinating colors; or use a theme to unify the pieces. Don't be upset if every line you paint is not perfect. No one will notice the imperfections but you. A foil doily works better than a paper one because it doesn't get soggy as quickly. Practice painting the doily on a piece of paper or scrap wood until you've mastered the technique.

Materials

Night table
Sandpaper
1-inch foam paintbrush
Latex primer paint
White semigloss enamel for top and lace
5 colors of 2-ounce bottles acrylic paints
Pencil

3 foil or paper doilies, cut in half
Roll of 1-inch-wide low-tack masking tape
¼-inch square-tipped paint-brush (wash brush)
Fine-tipped paintbrush (liner brush)
Water-based sealer

1. Remove hardware from table. Lightly sand and clean surface. Apply one or two coats latex primer. Let dry. Paint top with two or three coats of white enamel. Let dry between coats. Paint the rest of the table with base color. Let dry.
2. Position cut doily on front of table so it looks as if it were hanging from the top edge. Trace outer edge with pencil. Repeat on all sides. Paint doily area with one or two coats white enamel. Do not paint stripes in outlined areas.
3. Along sides of table, horizontally mark 1-inch intervals from top to bottom. Match and connect top and bottom marks with strips of 1-inch-wide masking tape on every other line. Paint exposed areas with second color of paint. Carefully remove tape. (Tape is removed before paint dries so that paint edges do not pull off with tape.) Let dry.
4. Along top and bottom, mark around table at 1-inch intervals. Place tape vertically between every other mark. Paint exposed areas with third color of paint. You will be painting over some previously painted horizontal stripes. Remove tape. Let dry.
5. With ¼-inch square-tipped brush, paint a vertical line with fourth color between wide stripes. Let dry. Paint a thin line, using fine-tipped brush with fifth color on each side of every other ¼-inch stripe.
6. Paint a thin line horizontally, using fifth color between every other wide stripe. Let dry.
7. Place cut doily on front of table over outlined area and hold in place with masking tape. Saturate foam brush with base color, blotting excess on paper towel. Gently paint over doily in downward strokes. Cover all open areas and around scalloped outlined edge. Dab brush in hard-to-cover areas. Remove doily. Repeat on other sides. Let dry. If you make a mistake while painting over doily, quickly wipe paint off with paper towel and start again.
8. Touch up stripes with small brushes where stripes and doily meet. Let dry. Cover plaid painted areas with two to three coats of water-based sealer.

Paper-Cord Lamp Base

A s I was shopping at the mall I passed a window display of large urns wrapped with sisal rope and I couldn't help thinking how lovely it would be to have a lamp made like that. When I got home I realized that paper cord found in crafts stores could be wrapped in the same way to make a colorful cover for the chipped lamp in my daughter's room. Paper cord comes in a wide variety of colors and is very inexpensive. The cord is wrapped around the lamp base and hot-glued along the bottom edge of the lamp. The hot glue will not damage a ceramic or glass lamp base, which makes this an ideal way to temporarily change your lamp to match the seasons or a holiday. I chose to use a few different colors of cord to coordinate with the color theme of the room, but one color wrapped around the lamp would look just as striking. There are many different textures you can use for wrapping—try yarn, twine, or satin cord; each will produce dramatically different results.

Materials

Lamp base
4 colors of paper cord, 2 yards of each to cover a small lamp base

Hot-glue gun and glue sticks
Scissors

1. To ensure that cord doesn't slip off bottom of lamp base, place a line of hot-glue along bottom edge of lamp base. Starting at center back, near electrical cord, lay paper cord on glue and press down. After going around lamp base once and reaching the center back, begin wrapping cord without any glue, going five times around base and ending at center back. Cut with scissors and hot-glue end to lamp base. **(Figure 1)**

2. Butt next color of cord end against first color end. Hot-glue to secure end and wrap around base five times, being sure to wrap tightly and keep level. Stop at center back. Cut and glue end to lamp base. Repeat, using all colors until lamp base is covered. If cord will not stay in place at indentations, secure with hot glue.

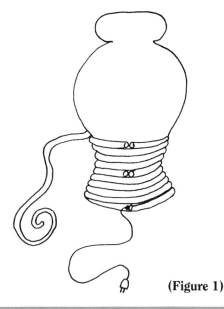

(Figure 1)

Shirred Lampshade Cover

These quick little shade covers can transform a plain or unsightly shade into a stylish one within minutes. Think of them as slipcovers for your lamps. They require very little fabric and can be made in half an hour. There is no sewing or complicated fitting involved. Choose a lightweight cotton or chintz with a light background so it doesn't darken the shade and obstruct the light. Look for interesting ribbons to tie on as an accent or use fishing line to tie the cover to the shade invisibly.

Materials

Lampshade
Fabric
⅜-inch-wide roll of iron-on
   adhesive or fabric glue
Large-eyed needle
Embroidery floss to
   match fabric or clear
   fishing line
Ribbon

1. To determine fabric yardage, measure shade from top to bottom and add 2 inches to measurement. Measure circumference at widest part of shade and multiply by two.
2. Lay fabric right side down. Fold all edges under ½ inch and press. Fold over another ½ inch and press. Fuse edges with iron-on adhesive or fabric glue.
3. Thread needle with floss and knot end. Starting from top left inside corner, sew a running stitch along top fold about ¼ inch below top edge. (If you want invisible stitches, use clear fishing line.) **(Figure 1)**
4. Place over lampshade and gather fabric. Double-knot ends of floss. Trim excess. Arrange gathers evenly around shade. Tie coordinating ribbon around top to hide stitches.

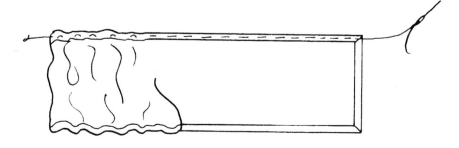

(Figure 1)

Striped Fan Blades

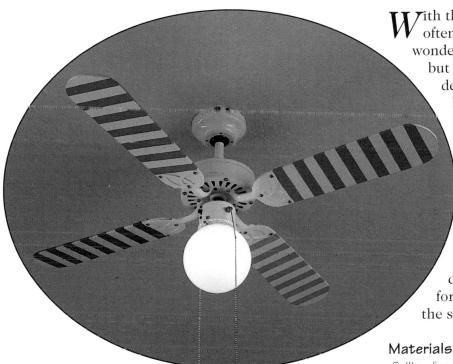

With this design you can add color where it is most often neglected—on the ceiling. Ceiling fans are wonderful when you do not have air-conditioning but can be eyesores when they don't fit into the decorating scheme. When my husband and I bought our home there was a dark-brown ceiling fan with antique brass fittings in each room. To make them less obvious, I painted each to coordinate with the room. When I was decorating my girl's room with a color-and-shape theme, I continued the palette by painting each blade in a different color of decorative stripes. The kids love to see it spin. The stripes were easy to paint using masking tape and a foam brush. For other designs, look for stencils especially designed for fan blades. I hung decorative pull cords in the shape of hearts to coordinate with the blades.

Materials

Ceiling fan with white blades
Pencil
Roll of 1-inch-wide masking tape

4 colors of 2-ounce bottles acrylic paints
Foam paintbrush
Water-based sealer

1. Remove fan blades from fan and clean thoroughly.
2. Starting from metal ornamental edge, use pencil to make marks at 1-inch intervals along both sides of blade. Repeat on all blades.
3. Place first piece of tape between first and second marks and around sides of blade. Then place tape at every other mark. The tip should have masking tape over it. Repeat on all blades.
4. Paint fan blade with two or three thin coats of acrylic paint in unmasked areas, remembering to paint sides of blades. Let dry between coats. Repeat with a different color on each blade. Let dry.
5. Remove tape. Brush one or two coats of water-based sealer on entire surface and side edges of blades. Let dry. Put blades back on fan.

Design Extra:
Stencil a circle of flowers on the ceiling around the base of a ceiling fan to resemble a plaster ceiling medallion.

Young Fire Fighter's Bedroom

*I*t is the accessories, not the big pieces of furniture that add charm and character to most rooms. This is especially true in children's rooms when a theme is used to coordinate the accessories. Color accessories placed in the right spot can make furniture look brighter and more interesting. All children have a favorite color, hobby, collection, or character that the room's accessories can reflect. Wallcovering companies offer many wallcoverings and borders to fit into a wide range of themes. The key to choosing the right accessories when using a theme is to build upon the theme and use restraint when choosing what parts of the room are to be accessorized. Instead of using just fire fighters or Dalmatians, the theme here is broadened to include everything associated with fire fighters. I used the color red, parts of a uniform, fire fighters' equipment, as well as Dalmatians. This adds the contrast needed to keep the room interesting and not overdone, while sparking a child's imagination.

Cardboard Valance

This valance uses cardboard from large appliance boxes that is cut to size, covered, and then stapled to the window molding. It is lightweight and a very inexpensive way of adding color to a window, especially in a boy's room where you may not want poufs and ruffles. I used fire-engine-red corduroy to cover the cardboard but an old rib-cord bedspread tucked away somewhere will cover the valance just as nicely. Be creative and cut the edges of the cardboard in scallops or in points, and cover with baseball pennants instead of fabric. Hot-glue any accents directly on the cardboard or fabric. If you don't have large boxes on hand, ask an appliance store clerk for extra boxes that may be available.

Materials

Fabric	Yardstick or T square
Cardboard from large appliance boxes or foam board from art-supply store	Pencil
	Scissors
	Wide masking tape
	Staple gun and staples
Utility knife	Paint to match fabric

1. Directions are for a single window valance. To determine fabric yardage, measure window width from outside edge of trim to outside edge of trim. Measure depth of projection and multiply by 2; add to window width measurement and use this width for valance. Use 15 inches for height. Add 4 inches to both width and height measurements to wrap fabric around the back of valance. (If there are any blinds or curtains, allow enough projection or clearance from wall to clear the existing rod, hardware, or curtains; 4 to 5 inches is usually sufficient).

2. Cut cardboard with utility knife using these measurements.

3. With yardstick or T square, mark the projection measurement on the back of the cardboard valance on each side. Draw a line from the top to bottom with pencil. Using point of closed scissors, score over line using edge of yardstick as a guide. Bend cardboard back at each scored line.

4. Lay fabric right side down. Center cardboard scored side up on fabric. Raw edges of fabric will be covered with masking tape. Wrap fabric taut around top and bottom. Use masking tape to secure fabric to cardboard. Fold sides over, making sure fabric on side pieces is smooth.

5. Paint a row of staples the color of fabric and let dry. Load into staple gun. Hold covered valance up to window with one edge against outer edge of window molding. Put two staples into cardboard and molding, one at top and bottom. Repeat on other side, making sure valance is placed straight across window.

Dalmatian Blinds

*I*ncorporating a theme into children's rooms stimulates their creativity and fuels their imaginations. Use their favorite toys or activities and apply throughout the room along with related objects. Inexpensive miniblinds take on the personality of the room when black spots to resemble a Dalmatian, the fire fighter's mascot, are applied. When the blinds are opened, the spots are partially hidden; when closed the spots come to life. Work on a large surface with a cutting board underneath. If you can't find black contact paper, spray-paint clear contact paper black and allow it to dry. Cover with another sheet of clear contact paper for protection, then cut into shapes.

Materials

Window blinds (minislat)
Black contact paper
Craft knife and extra blades

1. Cut contact paper in random-size ovals and circular shapes to look like spots.
2. Remove blinds and clean thoroughly. Put blinds on work surface in closed position. Stick black spots randomly over slats, being sure to press each spot firmly onto blind.
3. Following the lines between slats, cut through shapes with craft knife. Change knife blade when dull. Hang blinds.

Wooden-Bead Lamp Base

When you incorporate a particular theme into a child's room, don't forget to add a touch of it to the decorative accessories. This lamp was found packed away and forgotten in the attic. Cleaning restored it somewhat, but transforming it with paint and wooden beads made it a child's delight. For a little girl's room, use plastic beads or even simulated crystal beads. I chose to place the beads in a sequence according to color. Be creative and design an interesting pattern on the lamp base as the beads are placed on the string.

Materials

Lamp	String
Wooden beads, enough to cover base	Hot-glue gun and glue sticks

1. Remove shade from lamp and set aside. Knot one end of a piece of string long enough to go around lamp base plus 6 inches. String beads until you have enough to go around base once. Place a line of hot glue along bottom edge of base. Tie strand of beads onto base and press into glue. Trim excess string, making sure no string shows. Repeat process, omitting glue until you reach top of lamp base. (Hot glue is applied only on the bottom strand so beads don't slip off.)

Design Extra:
Hot-glue a few extra beads to the lampshade finial to accent the lamp.

Wallpaper-Border Lampshade Cover

If you use a wallpaper border in a room, use any left-over paper to make a coordinating lampshade. It will not only extend the colors throughout the room but adds a decorator touch to an ordinary lamp as well. If your lampshade is longer than the border, use a coordinating wallpaper cut to size. The cover is placed over an existing shade and tied on with decorative ribbon.

Materials

Lampshade
Wallpaper border or wallpaper cut to height of shade
Ruler
Pencil
Paper clip
Paper hole punch
¼-inch-ribbon, circumference of top of shade plus 15 inches
White glue

1. To determine amount of wallpaper border needed, measure bottom circumference of shade and multiply it by 2 for length; height of shade is height of paper needed.
2. Lay wallpaper printed side down. Using a ruler, measure ½ inch or pleat size you desire. Make a small mark with pencil. Continue marking at ½ inch intervals across top and bottom on entire length of wallpaper.
3. Lay ruler vertically to line up and connect the first two marks. Open a paper clip and use the point to gently score the wallpaper by running it lightly against the ruler. (Practice this on an extra piece of wallpaper. You do not want to go through the paper.) Continue to connect all pencil marks and score lines.
4. Turn wallpaper over and pleat as you would a fan.
5. Pinch sides of one pleat together, then using a paper punch, punch a hole about ¼ inch below top edge. Repeat for each pleat.
6. Thread ribbon through holes and tie over existing shade. Make a bow and trim excess. Arrange pleats evenly around shade. Glue edges together in back with white glue. If pleats do not lay flat, you may have too many; remove a few at a time and make sure each pleat has a crisp fold, or when pleats are arranged over existing shade, put a dot of hot glue under every few pleats to hold in place.

Design Extra:
Spray-paint a small section from a ladder bright yellow to complete the fire fighter motif. Prop against the bed or suspend from the wall for hanging stuffed animals.

CHAPTER FIVE

KITCHENS

"*No matter where I serve my guests it seems they like my kitchen best.*" *Anyone who entertains knows this all too well. An attractively decorated kitchen will become a happy place to gather at any time of the day. The kitchen of yesterday was used only for cooking. Kitchens today are a constant hub of activity and can be considered a family room as well. From a family breakfast to bill paying at noon, then homework on the table after school to a lone midnight raid on the refrigerator, the kitchen is rarely unoccupied. A kitchen has to be the most functional and organized room in a house full of busy people. Cabinets, counter space, reliable appliances, and proper lighting are necessities in every kitchen. The extras—cooking island, desk, and table—are the pieces we choose to fit our lifestyles. When choosing colors for the kitchen select those in harmony with the rest of the house to maintain a visual flow to the next room. Plenty of sunlight and bright colors always make a kitchen cheery. The rest is up to you.*

Country Kitchen

A warm and inviting kitchen is truly the heart of the home. It is where a family gathers not just for meals but to sit and relax and enjoy one another's company. The aroma of food baking in the oven reminds us of when we were children waiting patiently for the oven to open so we could sample the goodies. To create a special mood in a room, use accessories that hint of the room's activities. A basket with balls of yarn and knitting needles placed by a table or chair in a corner might suggest that this is a special place where you knit and relax, enhancing the room's appeal both for you and others. A country kitchen reflects a warm and cozy setting reminiscent of days gone by.

Reverse Window Swag

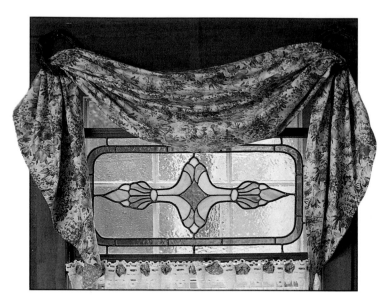

S wags are so easy to make, but they can look quite formal. Hanging them loosely on mini-grapevine wreaths is an excellent way of adapting them to a country setting. A swag is usually hung so the cascading edge of fabric falls toward the inside of the window. When the swag is placed so the cascading fabric falls to the outside, as shown here, it takes on a more whimsical appeal. The choice of fabric does not have to be limited to small prints or calicoes. A larger delicate floral pattern is a good choice in a room with barn siding, oak furniture, and handmade crafts.

Materials

Fabric	Yardstick
Coordinating fabric for lining	Pencil
Sewing gauge	Scissors
⅜-inch-wide roll of iron-on adhesive	2 mini-grapevine wreaths
	2 nails

1. Directions are for a single window. To determine fabric yardage for length, measure window width plus desired drop on each side of the window, adding 15 inches for draping. Width is 29 inches. To save on fabric yardage if you are making more than one window treatment, cut one width of fabric in half lengthwise.

2. Lay fabric and lining wrong sides together. Using a sewing gauge for accuracy, fold long edges over ½ inch on each piece and press. Place iron-on adhesive or fabric glue between the two pieces of fabric on the edge of the folds, making sure edges match. Press to fuse fabrics together. **(Figure 1)**

3. Lay fused fabric and lining with lining side down. On top edge, measure 24 inches in from each corner and make a small pencil mark. Place a yardstick diagonally on fabric to connect pencil mark to bottom outer corner. Draw a pencil line to each corner. With scissors, cut fabric through both thicknesses on pencil lines. **(Figure 2)**

4. Fold raw diagonal edges of fabric and lining under ½ inch and fuse together with iron-on adhesive to create a finished edge.

5. Hang wreaths on top corners of your window with small nails.

6. Lay swag face side up, with longer edge on bottom. Gather swag into folds and place each end through wreaths. Arrange length on each side as desired. Use your fingers to arrange swag in soft folds.

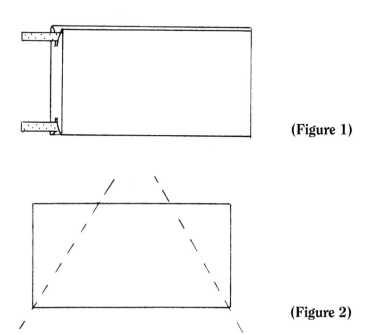

(Figure 1)

(Figure 2)

Cafe Rod Cover

Shifting attention to detail not only enhances the overall appeal of a room but adds immeasurable character, charm, and style as well. Details can be decorative and functional. Adding a special finishing touch is easily done by looking at every element in a room and thinking of something truly unique that transforms them from good-looking to exquisite. The rod cover adds a colorful finishing touch to purchased lace cafe panels, and makes them look custom-made.

Materials

Fabric
⅜-inch-wide roll of iron-on
    adhesive or fabric glue

1. To determine fabric yardage, measure window width and multiply by 2 for length; 5 inches is width.
2. Lay fabric right side down and fold both short edges and one long edge over ½ inch. Fuse short edges only with iron-on adhesive or fabric glue; press.
3. With fabric still right side down, fold both long edges to center, overlapping slightly so raw edge is under folded edge. Fuse. Slip rod through rod cover and gather on rod. Thread lace panels over covered rod.

Design Extra:

Cover lamp base with fabric and tie coordinating fabric in a bow around lamp neck. Hot-glue bow tails to lamp base every few inches to make them look like they're cascading down.

Scrap Fabric Chair-Back Cover

Chair back covers add color and help emphasize the style of a room. I improvised with iron-on adhesive and the fabric scraps from the diagonal cuts of the reverse swag project (see page 112). The scraps become a way of dressing up plain ladder-back chairs without sewing. I experimented with the idea only because I dared to try something different. By exploring the possibilities of adapting the remnants to my needs, I created something decorative that became one of the highlights of the room. The scraps from one swag will make one chair-back cover.

Materials

Fabric scraps from Reverse Window Swag project (see page 112)

⅜-inch-wide roll iron-on adhesive or fabric glue
Coordinating fabric or wide ribbon for bow

1. Directions are for one cover. The scrap of fabric should already be fused together with one face piece and one lining piece. Open fabric along fused seam, but do not separate the two pieces. You should have a triangular-shaped piece of fabric. **(Figure 1)**
2. Finish all the edges by folding under ½ inch. Fuse with iron-on adhesive or fabric glue and press. **(Figure 2)**
3. Wrap around chair so diagonal point is down, pulling taut. Overlap edges on opposite side, leaving enough to hem, overlap, and fuse. Cut away excess with scissors. Remove cover from chair. Fold one edge under ½ inch, fuse, and press. Put cover back on chair, pulling fabric taut with raw edges under folded edge. Use fabric glue to adhere the two edges of fabric together. **(Figure 3)**
4. Repeat on other side, using the other triangular scrap from the reverse swag and putting the second piece of fabric over the first piece. The pattern will be reversed on front and back of chair. **(Figure 4)**
5. Slide both sides up evenly about 1 ½ inches above top of chair. Wrap as you would the end of a package, overlapping edges slightly. Place a line of fabric glue between overlap and hold in place with pins a few minutes. Let dry.

If fabric won't hold shape, lay chair with cover on a towel and push top of chair against a wall covered with enough waxed paper to protect chair and wall while holding top in place until it dries to form a box-like top. Add a few stitches on top if necessary. **(Figure 5)**
6. Cut coordinating fabric for bow into a strip measuring 8½ inches by 72 inches (2 yards). Lay strip of fabric right side down. Fold one long edge over ½ inch and press. Fold both long edges to center, overlapping slightly so raw edge is under folded edge. Fuse and press. Tie into bow. Clip tails on an angle and turn edges inside fabric ¼ inch. Fuse and press.
7. Use strips of iron-on adhesive to attach bow to back of chair cover. Slide cover back onto chair.

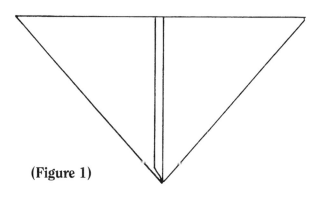

(Figure 1)

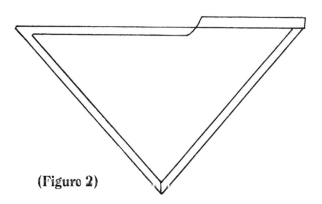

(Figure 2)

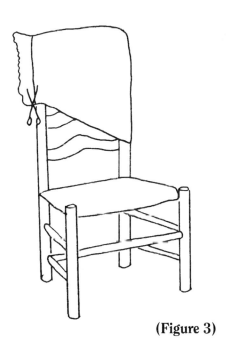

(Figure 3)

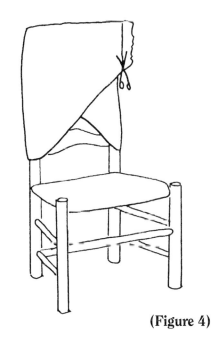

(Figure 4)

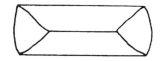

(Figure 5)

Design Extra:

Make a no-sew table topper. Cut a 28-inch square from fabric, folding all edges under ¹/₂ inch. Fuse with iron-on adhesive and press. Fuse ribbon or coordinating fabric with raw edges folded over ¹/₄ inch. Fuse to perimeter of the square.

Blue-and-White Kitchen

A blue-and-white kitchen looks crisp, clean, and bright. I began decorating with these colors when my collection of blue and white dishes, pottery, and porcelain accessories began to expand beyond my china cabinet. The colors from the dishes became the theme of my kitchen. Any collection displayed in an abundance of colors and textures gives depth and the illusion of substance, whether they're yard sale finds or priceless treasures. Decorating around that collection will provide great joy, especially when you thoroughly love what you collect. It will give meaning to your room and provide a commentary on your lifestyle, and make it a comfortable room you will enjoy for a long time.

Center-Pocket Window Valance

2. Lay fabric right side down. Fold all edges ½ inch to wrong side of fabric and press. Fold fabric in half lengthwise so edges meet and right side of fabric faces out. Press. **(Figure 1)**

3. Open fabric at center fold. Center your curtain rod on the fabric above fold line. With pencil, mark on fabric where rod is centered, allowing room for rod to slip through easily once seamed. Remove rod. Using a yardstick, measure from fold to first mark and note measurement. Then measure from fold to second mark and note measurement. Measure up from fold and mark first measurement every 12 inches across length of fabric. Repeat for second measurement. Connect all marks to make two separate lines with yardstick and pencil. **(Figure 2)**

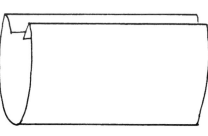

(Figure 1)

4. Place iron-on adhesive along outer edge of each line, then fold bottom half of fabric over it, matching top edges where fabric meets. Fuse and press. Fuse top edges together with iron-on adhesive. Let dry. Put valance on rod. Arrange gathers evenly across window.

A center-pocket valance adds color to a window, and allows maximum light to stream in to brighten the room. It is a perfect choice for a kitchen because the need for privacy is minimal. A valance will cost less to make because it requires less fabric than most window treatments. This center-pocket valance is simply a length of fabric folded with a center-pocket fused in for the rod. I used a 1 ¼-inch-wide conventional rod. To emphasize the center pocket of the valance even more, use a 3-inch-wide continental rod.

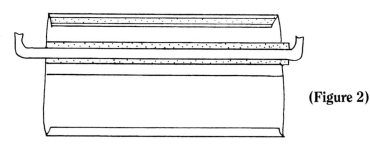

(Figure 2)

Materials

Fabric
Pencil
Yardstick

⅜-inch-wide roll of iron-on adhesive

1. To determine fabric yardage, measure window width from outside frame to outside frame and multiply by 2 for length; use 22 inches for fabric width. If you are using a wide (continental) rod, add width of rod to the fabric width (22 inches). Cut fabric to size.

Design Extra:
Hot-glue coordinating cord or braided trim to fabric above and below rod pocket. It will accentuate the center of the valance.

Painted Pitcher and Bowl

When I go to flea markets I always look for a blue-and-white pitcher and bowl, but I rarely find one that isn't too expensive. One time I stumbled upon a chipped and badly glazed green one that was the right shape and size, so I quickly bought it knowing I could change it with paint to resemble the one I wanted. This project stresses that the shape and size of things should never be overlooked because of a flaw if it can be altered in some way. Because of the pitcher's size it fills the empty space on the top of my cupboard beautifully. When I painted this one, I used regular acrylic paint and water-based sealer. Consider trying one of the new glossy acrylic paints available now that adhere to ceramic surfaces and can be washed without damaging the finish.

Materials

Pitcher and bowl set	Pie tin
Medium-grade sandpaper	Large sea sponge
2-inch foam paintbrush	Paper towels
White acrylic paint	Glossy water-based sealer
Blue acrylic paint	

1. Roughen surfaces of pitcher and bowl by sanding lightly. Clean surfaces thoroughly and let dry.
2. With foam paintbrush, brush on two coats of white acrylic paint, letting dry between coats.
3. Pour some blue paint into pie tin. Wet sponge with water and wring out. Dab sponge into paint and blot on a paper towel. Dab sponge on pitcher in random areas, turning sponge in different directions as you work around pitcher. Recoat sponge and blot, and continue to cover entire surface, making sure not to concentrate too much paint in any single area. Let dry.
4. Brush on two to three coats of glossy water-based sealer, letting them dry between each coat.

Design Extra: Spray-paint dried hydrangeas and place in pitcher for added color and texture.

Dish-Towel Stool Covers

Covering plain and inexpensive cushion-top stools bought at discount stores with fabric is a great way to add a splash of color and pattern to your decorating scheme. For extra charm, wrap a little skirt around the stool. There are sewing patterns, of course, but since I am not a seamstress I experimented with dish towels and iron-on adhesive to make terrific-looking covers. Dish towels are an inexpensive fabric choice, with finished edges that are extra handy. The top is permanently stapled on. The skirt is gathered on thread then tied and hot-glued onto the stool.

Materials

Stool with padded top
Three 20 x 27-inch or larger
   dish towels
Staple gun and staples
⅜-wide-roll of iron-on adhesive or fabric glue

Embroidery floss or yarn to
   match dish towel
Large-eyed sewing needle
45 inches of ½-inch round
   cord
Hot-glue gun and glue sticks

1. Cut dish towels as shown in Figure 1, creating one top piece, two ruffle pieces, two cord cover pieces, and two band pieces.

2. Center top piece on top of stool and staple underneath seat, pulling taut as you work around stool. Trim excess.

3. Turn the two ruffle pieces so the towel's manufactured finished edge is the bottom hem of ruffled skirt. Fold raw edges over ½ inch, fuse with iron-on adhesive or fabric glue, and press.

4. Matching pattern if necessary, fuse together the two ruffle pieces by overlapping manufacturer's finished edges with a 1-inch seam to create one long ruffle piece. **(Figure 2)**

5. Thread enough floss through needle to go around stool plus 10 inches and knot end. Sew a running stitch across top of ruffle piece. Gather fabric by pulling dish towel back on thread. **(Figure 3)**

6. Wrap floss around stool so top edge of ruffle and stool meet. Tie two ends of floss together to hold ruffle on stool. Trim any excess threads. Adjust fabric along floss so gathers are spread out evenly.

7. Place the two band pieces right side down. Fold long edges over 1 inch, fuse, and press. Matching pattern if necessary, fuse together the two band pieces by overlapping manufacturer's finished edges with a 1-inch seam to create one long band piece.

8. Lay the two cord-cover pieces right side down side by side, with edges overlapping slightly. Matching pattern if necessary, fuse together the two cord cover pieces by overlapping manufacturer's finished edges with a 1-inch seam to create one long cord-cover piece.

9. Center cord on wrong side of cord-cover piece and wrap fabric around cord so edges meet. Place a line of iron-on adhesive or fabric glue as close as possible to cord and press excess fabric that extends beyond cord. Repeat along entire length of cord. Let dry. **(Figure 4)**

10. Lay band piece right side down and lay cord cover on top of band piece so that cord is above top of band and excess cord-cover fabric lies on the band. Fuse or glue excess cord-cover fabric to band. Let dry. **(Figure 5)**

11. Wrap cord/band piece snugly around stool so cord is slightly above top of stool. Butt cord ends together and trim excess. Handstitch closed with floss. Put a line of hot glue into crevice between top of stool and cord to help hold in place. Let dry.

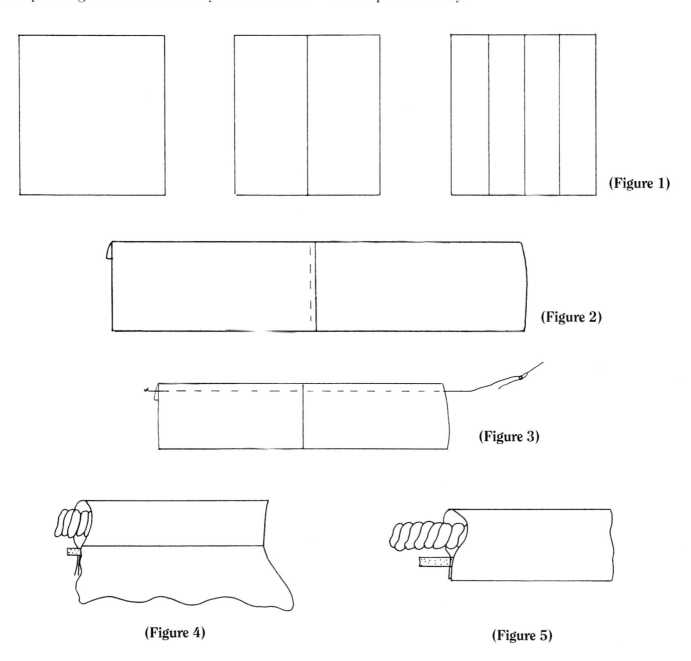

(Figure 1)

(Figure 2)

(Figure 3)

(Figure 4)

(Figure 5)

Hanging-Ladder Pot Rack

*I*nstead of discarding items that we no longer need, decorate with the environment in mind by extending the use of things beyond their original purpose. This philosophy came to mind when I salvaged an old bunk-bed ladder from curbside trash to make a functional hanging pot rack. Not only does the pot rack visually add character to the kitchen, it's also functional because it clears up cabinet space and makes room for something else. There are many options to use as hooks depending on the thickness of your ladder. The least expensive probably are rafter hooks, and the most expensive are those sold separately to go with a purchased rack. I painted my rack white because at the time I wasn't sure what look I wanted. Seeing it hang in my kitchen, I am better able to see what it needs to make it special and to fit it in with the rest of the room's decor. Now I am down to two options, sponging blue or stenciling. Add more country feeling to the rack with dried flowers and herbs, or place a large basket filled with flowers on the top.

1. Paint ladder with two coats of enamel. Let dry between each coat.
2. Lay ladder on work surface and drill a small hole in each end. Screw in screw eyes. **(Figure 1)**
3. Find ceiling joists. Mark on the ceiling with pencil to line up screw eyes with ceiling hooks. (The easiest way to do this is to have a friend hold the ladder against the ceiling while you mark the placement of the screw eyes.) Screw ceiling hooks in at pencil marks.
4. Hang one length of chain from each hook and attach to screw eye on ladder. Repeat at each corner.
5. Place rafter hooks over ladder for hanging pots and pans.

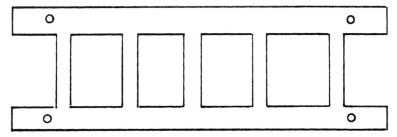

(Figure 1)

Materials

Small ladder cut to size
Semigloss enamel paint
Four 1-inch white screw eyes,
    spray-paint if necessary
Pencil
Four 2 ⅟₁₆-inch white screw-
    in ceiling hooks

4 lengths of white chain
    (length determined by
    how far ladder will hang
    from ceiling)
Rafter hooks (remove plas-
    tic covering if desired)

Design Extra:
Color and distress a basket by brushing basket with paint. Let dry for about 10 minutes, then wipe paint off to expose the bare basket stained with color. Rub with sandpaper to distress even more.

Gift Wrap-Covered Clock

Sometimes we find that as our decorating tastes change, our decorative accessories no longer fit into our decor even though they still work or are in good shape. Instead of replacing this clock, which used to have a dark walnut finish and beige face, I opted to decoupage it with gift wrap. This type of decoupage involves nothing more than cutting out strips of paper gift wrap and overlapping them to cover the surface.

The gift wrap can be a solid color or a pattern; no intricate design is needed. The new clockface was traced on heavy white paper with a black pen. Each clock will be unique in its construction. If your clock will not come out of its frame, you can first mask the face with tape to keep the decoupage medium from getting on it. For the cost of gift wrap, I now have a new clock to fit into my blue-and-white kitchen.

1. Carefully remove staples or nails from the back of clock using pliers. Remove glass and clockface from frame. Clean frame.
2. Cut gift wrap into rectangles, each about 1 x 2 inches in size.
3. Using foam paintbrush, brush back of first piece of gift wrap with decoupage medium and place under inner edge of frame and around to the front. Smooth with foam brush dipped in decoupage medium to remove wrinkles and air bubbles. Repeat around inner edge and front, overlapping each piece slightly. Continue to overlap pieces and work on front of frame, then around to outer edge and back. Around corners or edges, use brush to push gift wrap into any grooves and around corner edges.
4. Coat entire surface with two coats of decoupage medium. Let dry between each coat.
5. To change clockface, cut a small x in the center of white paper using a craft knife. Remove hands from clock; if they don't come off, position them together and slip hands through hole until paper lies flat on clock surface. Carefully trim excess paper around hole.
6. Using a fine-tipped marker, trace existing clockface and all the details you want to include.
7. Carefully remove paper and use spray adhesive on clockface, being sure not to get adhesive on clock hands. Carefully position paper back over center of clockface.
8. Smooth from center to outer edges, making sure no air bubbles or creases form. Trim outer edge with scissors. Staple or nail clockface and glass back into frame.

Materials

Clock	Craft knife
Needle-nose pliers	Decoupage medium
Gift wrap	Fine-tipped black marker
1-inch foam paintbrush	Spray adhesive
White paper, cut the size of clockface	Scissors
	Staple gun and staples

Design Extra: Cover any surface using this technique—including vases, picture frames, waste baskets, and even lamp bases.

BATHROOMS

*W*ith little effort a small, ordinary bathroom can become a beautiful place. A bathroom needs to feel spacious, be functional and visually appealing, but doesn't require an expensive overhaul to be luxurious as well. If the fixtures are in working order try to revive them with paint or colorful wallcovering. Use furniture and decorative touches you would normally reserve for other rooms in your home. Moisture can be a problem in some bathrooms, causing mildew and improper wallpaper adhesion. If so, a good exhaust system to remove excess moisture will alleviate the problem. Good organization is vital in most bathrooms. Check home centers for the many cleverly designed racks and storage units to keep personal products neatly hidden away. Then you'll have room for a few decorative objects to create a truly stylish bath.

Rediscovered Bath

*T*his bathroom was an eyesore to its owners, who always kept it out of sight behind a closed door. With a cosmetic face-lift, however, it became a favorite room. A cornice with a design of clustered violets on ribbons coordinates with the floral roller shade and sponged paint, as well as the multicolored stripe wallcovering. Designs were cut from leftover wallpaper and glued to camouflage exposed plumbing and highlight the bathtub. The inexpensive little details—lace hand towels, coordinating waste basket, pretty soaps in a glass dish, and towels rolled and stacked in white shelves—pile on the charm to make the room contrast dramatically with its dated and sterile origins.

Polystyrene Insulation Cornice

*M*ost cornices are made of wood that must be cut and when constructed, are heavy and difficult to manipulate. Polystyrene insulation is lightweight, very inexpensive, and easy to cut to size with a craft knife. The insulation is sold in home-improvement stores and comes in packages of eight to ten panels—enough for three or more cornices. The construction is easy, with only four pieces to glue together. Once decorated, it is then hot-glued onto angle irons that are mounted above the window. A cornice frames the top of a window, adding dimension and a punch of color without getting in the way. The height of this cornice is only nine inches, but you can change the size to fit your window and the amount of covering you desire. Another ideal place for a cornice is over a sliding glass door where vertical blinds are hung. A cornice adds a colorful accent to the wide-open space and doesn't get in the way of the sliding doors.

Materials

Wallpaper	Low-temperature glue gun
Polystyrene insulation	or white glue
panels	Large and small straight
Craft or utility knife	pins or T-pins
Pencil	Coordinating fabric
Yardstick or T square	2-3 angle irons

1. Measure window width from outside edge of molding to outside edge of molding and add 5 inches for cornice length; when cornice is positioned, it should wrap around the window. For width, measure height of wallpaper border and add 2 inches.

2. Lay insulation panel on flat surface or cutting board. Using a yardstick and pencil, mark dimensions for length and width just measured along length of insulation panel. Connect marks. Run a craft knife against edge of yardstick to cut through insulation. The insulation will snap apart easily. This is your front panel.

3. Cut two side pieces to height of front panel; length is determined by measuring depth from wall past any existing curtain rod or blinds. Four to five inches is usually sufficient. Add 1 inch for clearance.

4. Cut one top piece, length the same as the front panel; depth to match the length of side pieces. **(Figure 1)**

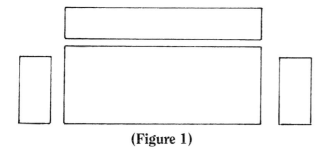

(Figure 1)

5. Put cornice together, using a low-temperature glue gun or white glue. If using white glue, let glue dry a few hours. Put large straight pins or T-pins in corner joints and seams for extra stability. **(Figure 2)**

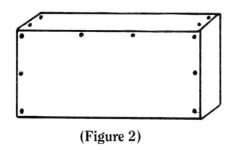

(Figure 2)

6. Cut fabric to size, using cornice measurements and adding 10 inches to each measurement. Lay fabric right side down. Center cornice so front panel is face down on fabric. Wrap fabric around cornice as you would a package, using straight pins pushed in on an angle to attach fabric to backside of cornice while pulling fabric taut. Miter the fabric at top corners so sides are smooth.

7. Center wallpaper border on front of cornice and bring around to both sides, pulling taut. Push straight pins on angle on inside of cornice sides.

8. Attach angle iron 2 inches from outside edge of molding and 1 inch from top of molding on each side of window. Place hot glue on top of angle irons. Center cornice on window and gently press cornice against wall and on angle irons. If angle irons have holes for screws, push a pin through cornice and into hole for extra stability. If your cornice is extra long, put a third angle iron over the center of the window for added support.

Construction Tips: If window is very wide, glue two panels of insulation together and brace at seam with two 3 x 6-inch pieces of insulation glued onto back. **(Figure 3)**

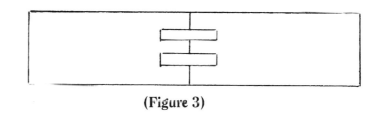

(Figure 3)

Design Extra:
For a padded cornice, line fabric with quilt batting first. Make swags and bows from extra fabric and pin to the front of cornice instead of using a wallpaper border.

Fabric Roller Shade

Roller shades offer an attractive alternative for a window where the fullness of curtains would get in the way. Shades are very economical and provide privacy. The only drawback is that they can leave a window looking stark. If you have a fabric shade you can fuse colorful fabric to it using less yardage than it would take to make curtains. Covering a shade with fabric to add color to a window is a better option than purchasing a solid-color shade to match the decor. Often, that solid color will clash with the exterior of the home. To present a nice exterior as well as interior image, cover the front of a neutral-colored shade. If you have a vinyl shade, keep the roller and purchase iron-on adhesive especially for making roller shades from a fabric store.

Materials

Fabric
Cloth roller shade (not vinyl)
Iron-on adhesive
Fabric stiffener or white glue
⅜-inch-wide roll of iron-on adhesive
Staple gun for wooden roller or heavy-duty masking tape for metal roller
Scissors
Foam paintbrush
Iron

1. To determine fabric yardage, remove shade from roller. Measure existing shade, adding 2 inches to width and 4 inches to length.

2. Cut fabric to size and press to smooth out any wrinkles. Remove slat from bottom of shade. Lay shade right side up and place iron-on adhesive over the entire shade. Press to fuse. Remove paper backing. Center fabric on shade right side up, allowing 1 inch extra on each side and 4 inches on bottom. Press to fuse fabric to shade. When fusing fabric to shade, start pressing from center out to all sides in small circular motions to avoid air bubbles. If air bubbles or wrinkles appear, gently remove fabric and repress or pop air bubbles with pin. The 1-inch extra fabric on each side will be cut off later to ensure non-fraying edges.

3. Brush fabric stiffener on side fabric edges, enough to cover the 1 inch of extra fabric on each side. Let dry. When shade edges are dry, turn shade to wrong side and trim excess fabric from sides using scissors for smooth, non-fraying edges.

4. Fold bottom edge of fabric over ⅜ inch; fuse with a strip of iron-on adhesive to make a finished edge. Fuse a ⅜-inch-wide strip of iron-on adhesive to wrong side of bottom edge of shade. Fold bottom edge of fabric to wrong side of shade 1 ½ inches and press to fuse.

5. Staple or tape shade back on roller, making sure it is straight.

Design Extra:
Make a small tassel (see page 29) to accent the bottom of the shade. Attach with hot glue.

Paint-Bucket Waste Can

The accessories you choose for a room are essential to successfully decorating it all the way down to the smallest detail. A bathroom wouldn't be functional without a waste can. But they can be unsightly. Dress up a five-gallon paint bucket or any cylinder-shaped can by covering it with shirred fabric. You will not only be helping the environment but you'll also accent a room with a large and attractive waste can. To change the decor, pull the fabric off and replace it.

Materials

5-gallon plastic paint bucket (cleaned and allowed to dry thoroughly)
Utility knife
2 ½ yards of fabric
Hot-glue gun and glue sticks

3 strips of coordinating fabric for braided trim, 3 inches wide and 144 inches (4 yards) long
⅜-inch-wide roll of iron-on adhesive

1. With utility knife, make a slit on each side of paint bucket where handle is attached; remove handle. Cut fabric 16 inches wide and 90 inches (2 ½ yards) long. **(Figure 1)**
2. Fold and press one long edge of fabric under 1 inch. This will be the finished edge placed along the top edge of the bucket.
3. Lay bucket on its side and lay fabric right side up with folded edge butted against the lip of the bucket. Position fabric so it is in front of you as you

(Figure 1)

work, leaving fabric clear of the bottom of the bucket. **(Figure 2)**
4. Move fabric away from top edge slightly and run a 5-inch line of hot glue on bucket where lip ends, not underneath lip. Quickly place the fabric over glue and push the fabric backward with your finger through the glue to shirr it. You can use a craft stick or wear a glove if the hot glue is too warm for your fingers. Repeat procedure around entire top edge until fabric edges meet, allowing 1 inch extra to fold under and make a finished edge; cut away excess fabric. **(Figure 3)**
5. Repeat above procedure along bottom edge, but pull fabric taut from top to bottom then fold under before gluing. **(Figure 4)**
6. To make braided trim from coordinating fabric, place each strip right side down. On each strip, fold long edges to center, overlapping slightly. Fold short ends under ¼ inch and fuse with iron-on adhesive. Braid the three strips together so overlapped seam of each strip is at the back. Wrap around bucket two times and tie in front. Trim ends.

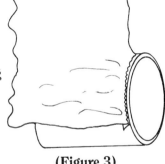

(Figure 2)

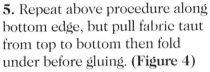

(Figure 3)

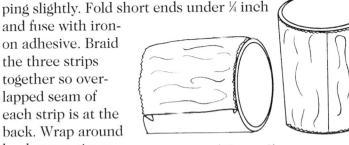

(Figure 4)

Design Extra:
In place of braided trim, wrap a ribbon around the bucket and tie in a decorative bow.

CHAPTER SEVEN

PORCHES

A porch is more than an entrance to your home. It sets the mood and can create a memorable first impression. Front, side, or back of the house, a porch is a transition from the outside world to the welcoming warmth of your home. In the summer months a porch can be considered a room that links the house to the yard and can be transformed into usable living space by decorating as comfortably and attractively as the interior of the home. Best of all, a porch can be a place to relax closer to nature, shaded fom the sun or protected from an afternoon shower while enjoying the pleasures of entertaining or the solitude of a good book.

Victorian Porch

*T*his porch is surrounded by color from a flower garden, which makes it so inviting. But don't stop there, bring the garden up on the porch with lots of flowers placed in decorative containers. Place a round piece of glass on a bird bath, add some lace and voila! You have an instant table suitable for the outdoor environment. Pretend your porch is a grand veranda from a bygone era and grace it with airy wicker furniture highlighted with lush colored fabrics. You might just see a cricket game begin on your lawn. A porch is the perfect place to unwind after a stressful day, enjoy the outdoors, and watch the sunset in the evening.

Stenciled Area Rug

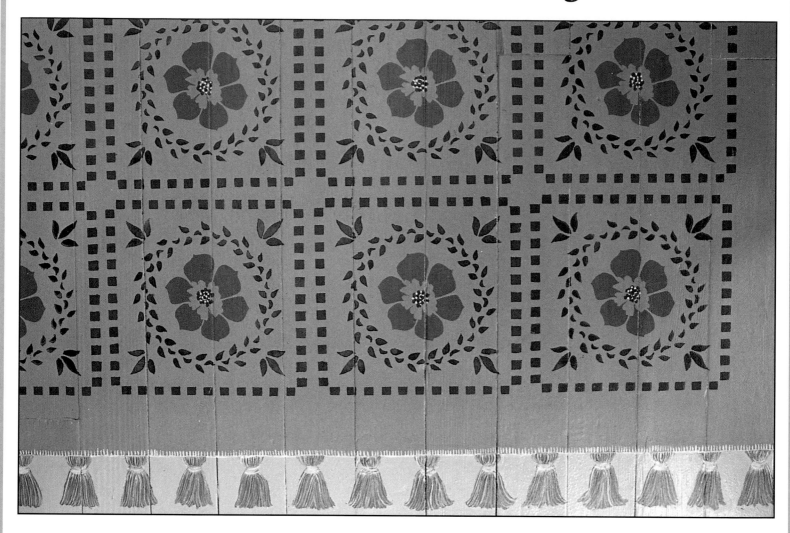

*I*s a real rug always getting underfoot? Or would you like a rug outdoors but know it won't live up to the elements. A trompe l'oeil rug is one way to solve the problem, and if it is placed where a real one would normally be, it will really fool the eye. If you have stenciled before, this project should be fairly easy. Choose the colors for your rug by selecting colors from fabrics in the room. The stencil design is a repeat of the same block of squares. I cut my stencil out using purchased stencil blanks. Clear acetate sheet protectors sold at office-supply stores work well as an inexpensive substitute. When tracing the pattern, remember to always make registration marks using dotted lines; this will tell you exactly where to place the next overlay of the design. To make cutting the stencil easier, change the knife blade often and cut on a glass surface (glass from a picture frame works well). When stenciling, always blot the brush on a paper towel first to absorb excess paint. This will keep the paint from bleeding under the stencil and give you expert results. Before starting, make sure floor surface is clean, sanded, and primed or in good shape with no visible signs of chipping or peeling.

Materials

Cutting surface
Four 10 x 10-inch stencil
   blanks or sheets of
   acetate
Low-tack masking tape
Thin-tipped black permanent
   marker
Ruler
Craft knife and extra blades
Chalk line or T square
Exterior paint primer (if paint-
   ing over an oil-based paint,
   use a gripping primer)
Stain killer (prevents any
   previous stain or varnish
   from bleeding through and
   changing paint colors)
Exterior paint for base color
   of rug
5 colors of acrylic paint
   (2-ounce bottles sold in
   craft stores)
Pie tin
Stencil brush
Fine-tipped paintbrush
Nonyellowing polyurethane

1. Enlarge design on photocopier to a 9-inch square or desired size. Ask at copy shop to use their proportional scale to figure out the size of enlargement you will need to fit the area you are planning to use for the rug. Make two copies. **(Figure 1)**

2. On cutting surface, tape one copy of design down and tape a piece of acetate over it. Make sure design and acetate are straight and square. Using a permanent marker and ruler, draw all small squares from design onto acetate. Remove acetate and cut out each square with craft knife.

3. Tape second piece of acetate over design and draw all the leaves. It is important to make registration marks. Draw two squares from each corner using dotted lines. Do not cut out these squares; they will be your placement guide when you start to overlay the stencil.

4. Tape third piece of acetate over design. Draw flower petals. Following the procedure in Step 3, use the four sets of corner leaves for registration marks. Remove acetate. Cut out petals.

5. Tape fourth piece of acetate over design and draw center of flower. Use the flower petals for registration marks; remove acetate and cut out center of flower.

6. To paint floor, measure area you want to cover, leaving a 2-inch border on all sides and ¼ inch between squares. Decide how many squares will fit across and lengthwise on the floor. Mark the length and width with a pencil and connect the lines with a chalk line or use a T square to make the outline of the rug straight and even on all sides. Place low-tack masking tape next to lines.

7. Paint floor with one or two coats of primer. Let dry between coats. If you are working on a floor that has been previously stained, apply one or two coats of stain killer in place of primer. Let dry between coats. Do not let paint dry completely with tape still down, or some of the paint edges might be stripped when you remove the tape. The masking tape should be removed 15 minutes after each coat of paint. Put new tape down for each new coat of paint.

8. Roll on two coats of base color. Let dry.

9. Starting at lower left hand corner, place stencil with squares 2 inches up and 2 inches over from corner, making sure it is straight. Secure in place with masking tape. Pour paint for squares into pie tin. Dab brush in paint and blot on paper towel. Stencil squares. Remove stencil carefully and position so squares for next block will be ¼ inch away. Repeat process until entire rug area is covered. Let dry completely.

10. Using registration marks, secure leaves stencil in place and stencil leaves inside center of first block of squares. Repeat for all blocks. Let dry completely.

11. Position and tape stencil with flower petals in center of first block. Stencil flower petals. Repeat for all blocks. Let dry completely.

12. Position and tape stencil with flower center on first block. Stencil flower center. Repeat for all blocks. Let dry completely.

13. Using fine-tipped paintbrush, paint dots in center of each flower. Paint small lines on each end of rug to resemble a bound edge. Trace tassel pattern onto floor or draw a row of 5 ½-inch-long tassels on each end of rug with primer. Let dry. Using fine-tipped brush, draw different-color strands through each tassel. Let dry completely. **(Figure 2)**

14. Cover with four or five coats of nonyellowing polyurethane, letting dry completely between each coat. Cover each tassel separately with polyurethane.

(Figure 1)

(Figure 2)

Wicker Skirt and Cushion Cover

1. To determine fabric yardage for cushion, measure cushion width, length, and depth, then multiply each by **2**. Add extra to pin fabric to underside of cushion. For skirt, measure circumference of love seat and double desired length of skirt; add 2 ½ inches to the skirt length measurement. For the trim and bow, measure circumference of the love seat plus 1 yard for the bow length and use 5 inches for width.

2. Lay fabric for cushion right side down. Center cushion on fabric and wrap taut around cushion as you would a package. Pin excess fabric on underside with safety pins to hold in place.

3. Lay fabric for skirt right side down. Fold top and bottom edges over ¼ inch and press. Fold over again 1 inch and fuse with iron-on adhesive or fabric glue to make a finished edge and hem. Thread needle with floss and knot end. Sew a 2-inch running stitch along top edge. Gather skirt fabric. Tie skirt around love seat with floss to arrange gathers evenly around love seat. Use hot glue or hook and loop fastener to attach skirt to love seat.

4. Lay strip for trim and bow right side down. Cut off 1 yard to use for bow; remaining fabric is for trim. Fold long edges of each piece toward center, slightly overlapping. Use iron-on adhesive or fabric glue to fuse seam. Tuck ends into each strip and fuse. Tie bow piece into a bow. Wrap trim strip around love seat to hide floss and hot-glue ends to back of skirt. Place some hot glue on each corner so trim stays in place. Hot-glue bow to center front of love seat.

W̶icker furniture looks so inviting on a porch. It makes you want to sit down and have a cool glass of lemonade on a hot summer day while watching the kids run through the sprinkler. A gathered skirt and colorful cushion on the love seat make the porch even more inviting by adding a touch of softness. Further enhance this effect by adding a few throw pillows. Personalize the rest of the wicker furniture by accenting each piece with strips of coordinating fabric or ribbon woven through an open pattern in the wicker.

Materials

Fabric
Coordinating fabric for bow
Seat cushion for love seat
3 large safety pins
Roll of iron-on adhesive

Large-eyed needle
1 skein of embroidery floss
Hot-glue gun and glue sticks
   or sticky-back hook and
   loop fastener

Design Extra:
Wrap unsightly plastic flowerpots with coordinating fabric. Center pot on wrong side of fabric and bring ends up, then put a rubber band over fabric and around top of pot. Roll excess fabric under rubber band to make a decorative edge.

Soda-Bottle Candle Lanterns

Recycle plastic soda bottles to make attractive and environmentally safe lanterns for your porch or yard. You can stencil them or use a hole punch to make a design around the top edge. Place in flowerpots, gardens, or along an entrance path. For an outdoor party, use citronella candles to repel bugs and add ambiance after dark. Save broomsticks when you replace an old broom to use as a pole. As with any lighted candle, do not leave unattended.

1. For each lantern: Cut broom off stick. Apply two or three coats of paint to cover stick. Let dry.
2. Cut soda bottle 4 inches below top. Remove aluminum band around neck. Trim cut edge to make even.
3. Hold cut portion of bottle so narrow (mouth) section is down and cut edge up. Stencil a pattern on outside of cut bottle. Let dry.
4. Place hot-glue around top edge of broomstick. Place mouth section over stick and press down into glue. If broomstick is too thick, chisel with knife.
5. Wrap paper cord around screw indents of bottle, starting and stopping in the same area. This will be the back where ends of cord meet. Hot-glue cord ends to bottle. Put a little bit of sand in bottom of candle holder and place candle inside.

Materials

1 broomstick
Acrylic paint
One 1-liter plastic soda
    bottle
Stencil and stencil brush
    (optional)

Hot-glue gun and glue
    sticks
Twisted paper cord
Sand
Votive candle

Design Extra:
Use masking tape to paint colorful stripes around the broomstick, or wrap paper cord around the entire broomstick. Tie a large bow with tails around lantern neck with ribbon.

Country Painted Floor

*F*resh paint in a display of colors mixed with a sten-ciled border transform a drab porch floor into some-thing special. The ease of this project comes from not having to put masking tape down to paint the squares. Instead, I used a rectangular car-wash sponge that is molded to fit the hand grip. Using a sponge produces a unique textural effect that makes the floor look dis-tressed. I stenciled a border all around, using a precut purchased stencil; I also accented every other square. Each square is 12 x 12 inches, but you can reduce or enlarge the size to fit your needs.

Materials

Sandpaper or electric sander	4 thumbtacks
Paint primer	String and chalk to make chalk line
Flat latex paint for base coat	Cardboard square cut to size
Purchased stencil	
Acrylic paints for stencil design	Pencil
Stencil brush	Paint roller and tray
Masking tape to hold stencil	Rectangular carwash sponge
	Nonyellowing polyurethane

1. Sand, prime, and paint floor with one or two coats of base color using paint roller. Let dry.
2. Using the purchased stencil, acrylic paints, stencil brush, and masking tape, paint a border around edge of floor, starting and ending in least-viewed area. Let dry.
3. Measure length and width of room from edge of sten-ciled border. Mark center of each wall at baseboard height. Mark center of room by drawing perpendicular lines across center of floor. To make sure your design will be straight, thumbtack the end of a piece of string to one mark on wall and stretch string across floor to mark on opposite wall. Repeat on other two walls. Rub chalk on strings. Snap string on the floor to leave a chalk mark.
4. Cut a 12-inch square or desired size from cardboard. Center diagonally over intersected lines so corners align with the pencil lines. Trace around square with pencil.

Continue drawing squares along pencil lines in center of room, matching corners of each square. Fill in the rest of the floor using center squares as guides and matching cor-ners. **(Figure 1)**
5. Mark a small x in alternating squares. Pour paint for squares in paint tray. Wet sponge and wring out. Dab sponge in paint and blot on paper towel. Align edge of sponge along inside lines of each square and press down, being sure to create a straight edge. Repeat to frame inside of square. Fill in center by dabbing sponge up and down. Repeat in all squares with x's.
6. Use a section from stencil design to stencil on intersect-ing corners of sponged squares. Let dry.
7. Finish floor with three or four coats of nonyellowing polyurethane, letting each coat dry completely.

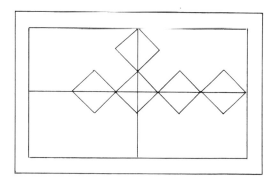

(Figure 1)

Suppliers

Spring Living Room
page 22
Tufted Ottoman: At Home in Charleston Collection fabric from York Wallcoverings and Fabric, 750 Linden Avenue, York, PA 17404

page 25
Fabric-Covered Lamp Base: At Home in Charleston Collection fabric from York Wallcoverings and Fabric

page 26
Poufy Tabletop: At Home in Charleston Collection fabric from York Wallcoverings and Fabric

page 30
Cardboard Shelf Backdrops: Mahogany Collection fabric from York Wallcoverings and Fabric

Summer Living Room
page 32
Cord rug: Pottery Barn, P.O. Box 7044, San Francisco, CA 94120

page 34
Sheet-Covered Sofa with Tassels: Imperial Damask sheets by Adrienne Vittadini, Fieldcrest Cannon, 1271 Avenue of the Americas, New York, NY 10019

page 35
Sheet-Covered Wing Chair: Imperial Damask sheet by Adrienne Vittadini, Fieldcrest Cannon

page 38
Wallpaper Pleated Shades: Lake Forest Collection wallpaper from York Wallcoverings and Fabric

page 41
Shirred Lampshade: Ginger Tree Collection fabric from York Wallcoverings and Fabric

page 43
Flange-Edged Pillow: Ginger Tree Collection fabric from York Wallcoverings and Fabric

Autumn Living Room
page 44
Round crocheted tablecloth: Domestications (catalog), P.O. Box 40, Hanover, PA 17333. 800-782-7722

page 44
Cord rug: Pottery Barn

Winter Living Room
page 52
Pillows: Old World Candlewicking in Black and Burgundy from Waverly 79 Madison Avenue, New York, NY 10016; Table skirt: Village Quilt Linen in Parchment from Waverly; Horsevane: Sturbridge Yankee Workshop, P.O. Box 9797 Porland, ME 04104; Cord rug: Pottery Barn

page 54
Fabric-Covered Sofa with Pleated Skirt: Old World Linen in Forest fabric from Waverly

page 56
Fabric-Covered Wing Chair: Black Watch fabric from Waverly

page 57
Shirred Curtain Rod with Tennis-Ball Finials: Firestone Linen in Forest fabric from Waverly

page 58
Flounced-Heading Curtains: Firestone Linen in Forest fabric from Waverly

page 60
Pleated Lampshade Cover: Glosheen Black fabric from Waverly

page 65
Wrap Pillow: Linsay in Claret fabric from Waverly Victorian Living Room

page 66
Striped wallpaper: Yorktown Collection from York Wallcoverings and Fabric

page 68
Throw Swags with Rosettes: At Home in Charleston fabric from York Wallcoverings and Fabric

page 69
Tablecloth Curtain: Amanda Lace tablecloth from Domestications (catalog)

Dining Rooms
page 76
Wallpaper border: Middlesex Collection from York Wallcoverings and Fabric

page 80
Knotted Chair-Back Slips: Lake Forest Collection fabric from York Wallcoverings and Fabric

page 81
Chandelier Chain Cover: Lake Forest Collection fabric from York Wallcoverings and Fabric

Bedrooms
page 87
No-Sew Balloon Shades: Poise 'n' Ivy Collection fabric from Three Sisters Studio, York

page 89
Piano-Bench Skirt: Poise 'n' Ivy Collection fabric from Three Sisters Studio

page 90
Ruched Cord and Bow Pillow: Country Inn at Meadowbrook Collection fabric from York Wallcoverings and Fabric

page 92
Ceiling-fan pull chains: Tender Heart Treasures, LTD. 1-800-443-1367

page 97
Fabric-Padded Headboard: Mahogany Collection fabric from York Wallcoverings and Fabric

page 100
Shirred Lampshade Cover: Mahogany Collection fabric from York Wallcoverings and Fabric

Kitchens
page 112
Reverse Window Swag: Country Inn at Meadowbrook Collection fabric from York Wallcoverings and Fabric

page 113
Cafe Rod Cover: Country Inn at Meadowbrook Collection fabric from York Wallcoverings and Fabric

Bathrooms
page 130
Fabric Roller Shade: A Cottage in Weatherby Woods Collection fabric from York Wallcoverings and Fabric

Porches
page 134
Flowerpot covers: Ginger Tree Collection from York Wallcoverings and Fabric; Pillows: Middlesex Collection from York Wallcoverings and Fabric

page 139
Wicker Skirt and Cushion Cover: Middlesex Collection fabric from York Wallcoverings and Fabric

page 141
Stencils: Makin'-It, Inc., 4281 Melbourne Court, Tucker, GA 30084. 404-491-8017

Etcetera
page 48
Basket for lamp by Pat Parenteau Eisemann

page 120
Trompe l'oeil by Gabby Barrett

Index

All of us at Meredith® Press are dedicated to offering you, our customer, the best books we can create. We are particularly concerned that all of our instructions for making projects are clear and accurate. Please address your correspondence to Customer Service Department, Meredith Press, 150 East 52nd Street, New York, NY 10022.

If you would like to order additional copies of any of our books, call 1-800-678-2803 or check with your local bookstore.